The Mexican-American War

A Captivating Guide to the Armed Conflict between the United States of America and Mexico along with the Impact of the Texas Revolution

Free Bonus from Captivating History
(Available for a Limited time)

Hi History Lovers!

Now you have a chance to join our exclusive history list so you can get your first history ebook for free as well as discounts and a potential to get more history books for free! Simply visit the link below to join.

Captivatinghistory.com/ebook

Also, make sure to follow us on Facebook, Twitter and Youtube by searching for Captivating History.

Contents

Introduction

The war between Mexico and the United States of America is among the list of wars that, despite its irrefutable importance, are not relatively well-known. Even though it was a major war that influenced the developments in North America for years to come and whose effects are still prevalent today, it sometimes can get overshadowed when people talk about the history of the world. The significance of the Mexican-American War can be overlooked when comparing it to other events of the 19th century, such as the Napoleonic Wars, Latin American wars for independence, or the unification of Germany and Italy. While all these occurrences are vital to understanding world history and were all impactful in their own right, the Mexican-American War just does not get the credit that it deserves. In the history textbooks of many non-US students, for example, almost no pages are dedicated to it, although they do talk about other wars that took place around the same time, such as the American Civil War.

However, the Mexican-American War had pretty relevant immediate and long-lasting consequences. It solved the territorial disputes between the two countries and helped shape the political geography of the continent; plus, it served as a triumphant victory of the expansionist US at the time, inspiring it to continue its efforts to "manifest" its "destiny." It also sent Mexico into a further period of instability and economic ruin, and, last but not least, it had a socio-cultural impact on both countries, especially with the matter of slavery in the US, which eventually led to the Civil War.

This book will cover every important aspect of the Mexican-American War. It will provide an in-depth look into its causes, from the most apparent ones, like the Texas Revolution, to ones that may not be clear at first glance, like the era of post-colonialism. It will also explore the pre-war states of both nations, as their analysis is crucial to the understanding of the grounds for the war. In addition, it will follow the war chronologically, from its declaration to its end with the Treaty of Guadalupe Hidalgo. We will examine the main actors, battles, and important events that took place over the course of the war's nearly three-year period. Furthermore, the book will elaborate on the numerous short- and long-term outcomes of the war to find out what changed after its completion. Finally, these pages will try to explain the phenomenon that caused the tendency of "pushing" the Mexican-American War to the side and underline its significance in world history.

Chapter 1 – The Effects of Colonialism and the Mexican War of Independence

Colonialism in The Americas

The age of colonization marked one of the most influential periods in world history. After the late 15th century, several European powers set their eyes, and therefore their sails, to the west. The New World promised indescribable riches, and Europeans went there to get a hold of them. Spain, Portugal, France, and Great Britain started landing on previously unexplored shores of what would later become North and South America. The indigenous peoples that they encountered posed little to no resistance. Technologically speaking, they were less superior, as they did not have access to advanced weaponry like steel armor and gunpowder. The colonists first defeated and later incorporated these people in their newly established settlements, taking the New World by storm.

In fact, both nations that took part in the Mexican-American War were, at some point in their existence, colonies of the Old World. The United States managed to gain its independence from the British in 1776, about seventy years before the start of the war. Mexico, on the other hand, became independent in 1821, about forty-five years after the US. While both events are important and interesting in their own right, it can be argued that Mexican independence is more relevant for understanding the Mexican-American War. This is not only due to Mexico's relative novelty in comparison to its counterpart but also because it was still struggling to overcome the sociopolitical difficulties it faced after gaining independence, which was contrary to the US, which had clearly set its goals and formed its identity as a dominant power in the region.[1] However, to better understand exactly how Mexico became independent, it is important to dive deep into the roots of Spanish colonialism and briefly look at New Spain—the biggest of Spain's colonies and what would later become Mexico.

New Spain

New Spain was one of the viceroyalties of the Spanish throne. This technically made the territory its own country and not a colony. The Viceroyalty of New Spain was governed by the viceroy, who was appointed by the Spanish monarch. New Spain still directly served the Kingdom of Spain. By the early 1800s, the viceroyalty had claimed lands that made it far larger than Mexico is today. It stretched from the modern-day southwestern US north to California all way to Central America. It even included parts of northern South America and some Pacific Ocean archipelagos, most notably the Philippines.[2] Of course, it was nearly impossible for a single viceroy to control such a vast area. Because of this reason, the territory was divided into several *audiencias*—courts of appeal that represented royal authority in different provinces and answered to the viceroy. *Audiencias* were probably the most important of the administrative divisions of New Spain because they were the largest and incorporated other smaller divisions, such as the *cabildos* and *intendencias*.[3] Mexico City was the

---

[1] Delay, Brian. (2007). "Independent Indians and the U.S.-Mexican War." The American Historical Review, 112(1), 35–68. http://www.jstor.org/stable/4136006.

[2] "Viceroyalty of New Spain (historical territory, Mexico)." Encyclopedia Britannica. Retrieved 14 October, 2021.

[3] Parry, J. H. (1940). "The Audiencia of New Galicia in the Sixteenth Century." Cambridge Historical Journal, 6(3), 263–282. http://www.jstor.org/stable/3020752.

capital and the heart of the nation; it became the largest city in the Western Hemisphere by 1800.

The population of New Spain was divided heavily among different classes. The system had been developing since the early colonial days, and it assigned privileges to its members based on their racial background. At the top were the *peninsulares*, who consisted of Spaniards that were born in Spain. The name refers to their origin of the Iberian Peninsula. Since *peninsulares* were at the top of the ladder, they enjoyed the economic and political privileges that came with being born in Europe and exercised their power over the lower classes. After them came the criollos, people who were born into *peninsular* families in the Americas. The criollos were also a privileged group, except for the fact that, unlike the *peninsulares*, they could not hold positions in the more important administrative offices. Below them were the *indios*, people who were solely of Native American descent, and the *mestizos*, which included people with one Spanish and one native parent. Both of these groups were closely intertwined, with most of them working as artisans and local shopkeepers. However, they had divisions among themselves too, with the *indios* sub-group that were the descendants of Aztec nobility enjoying distinctively more privileges than the commoners, who constituted most of the population.[4] At the bottom of the caste system stood the offspring of Africans and Europeans, who did not have any real benefits and lived mostly in poverty, and the people of purely African descent, who were mainly brought to New Spain during the colonial slave trade.[5] However, differently from their US neighbor, the Spaniards did not really practice slavery at the turn of the 19th century. Even though it was still legal in the country, New Spain's market consisted mostly of higher-paid jobs like textile and dye

---

[4] L. N. Mcalister. "Social Structure and Social Change in New Spain." Hispanic American Historical Review 1 August 1963; 43 (3): 349–370. doi: https://doi.org/10.1215/00182168-43.3.349

[5] [Anon.] (2001). "Sociolinguistic stratification in New Spain." 2001 (149), 55-78. https://doi.org/10.1515/ijsl.2001.023

manufacturing. This ensured the growth and the prominence of the *mestizo* class, who were essentially the middle class, and thus significantly reduced slavery.

Finally, the third most important aspect in understanding how the Viceroyalty of New Spain functioned has to be its religion. Spain was a devoted Roman Catholic nation and had remained so despite the Protestant Reformation, which had transformed the religious landscape of Europe several hundred years before. The original conquest of the Americas by Spanish conquistadors included spreading Catholicism as the prominent faith among the indigenous peoples of the New World. The native population was extremely religious in their own regard, but by the 1800s, almost all of New Spain had been converted. The natives became firm believers of Catholicism and often incorporated symbolism and imagery from their old religions. The most prominent example of this merging of the two cultures is probably the legend of the apparition of the Virgin Mary, now referred to as the Lady of Guadalupe, to an indigenous farmer in 1531. Since then, it has become a religious symbol, and she is the patroness of all of Catholic Latin America.[6] This, paired with an already well-established institution that was the Catholic Church in New Spain, provided for one of the foundations of the colony's existence.[7]

It was these three aspects—the administrative, social, and religious order—that guaranteed the well-being of New Spain. The nation was built upon the fundamental concepts of it being a part of the Spanish Crown, its clear-cut distinctions between the different social strata and the privileges that came with it based on race, and its whole-hearted devotion to Catholicism. Understanding how New Spain functioned

[6] Wolf, E. R. (1958). "The Virgin of Guadalupe: A Mexican National Symbol." The Journal of American Folklore, 71(279), 34–39. https://doi.org/10.2307/537957

[7] Palfrey, Dale Hoyt. (1998). "Religion and society in New Spain: Mexico's Colonial era." Retrieved from https://www.mexconnect.com/articles/1562-religion-and-society-in-new-spain-mexico-s-colonial-era

before Mexico gained its independence is crucial to determining and analyzing the events that were the direct consequences of change and perhaps even, to an extent, the failure of its three principles. New Spain would last for as long as these pillars stood firm.

The Spread of Revolutionary Ideas in New Spain

It was the events that took place in Europe at the end of the 18th and the beginning of the 19th centuries that prompted the spread of revolutionary ideas in New Spain, just as it did in places like Latin America and most of Europe. Of course, the main occurrence during this time was the French Revolution of 1789 and Napoleon Bonaparte's subsequent rise from the ranks of a talented French general to the emperor of France. Napoleon's conquests "liberated" the nations of Europe from the tyrannical rule of their monarchs and promoted the principles of liberty, equality, and fraternity. His efforts did not only have significant results in Europe; his conquest of Spain also started nationalistic movements all throughout the Spanish colonies, including the revolution in Mexico. In 1808, after about a year of war with the Spanish, Napoleon forced King Charles IV and his son Ferdinand VII to abdicate. He then installed his brother, Joseph Bonaparte, as the new ruler of Spain. Even though Spain continued to resist Napoleon's conquest for years to come, the act was enough for the colonies to question the legitimacy of the Spanish Crown in their territories. For them, the viceroy was the "king's living image."[8] So, if there was no legitimate Spanish ruler on the throne, then who were they supposed to answer to?

Before the crisis on the mainland, the situation in New Spain was not stable either, to say the least. The Spanish Crown had introduced new policies to consolidate its hegemony in the region and ensure the power of the Catholic Church. These policies were implemented in order to grow the income of the viceroyalty. They mainly changed the

---

[8] Cañeque, Alejandro. *The King's Living Image: The Culture and Politics of Viceregal Power in Colonial Mexico*. New York: Routledge, 2004.

terms of loans given out to the locals by the church and forced the borrowers to pay enormous amounts of money that they didn't possess. Since most of the loans were held by the criollos, the reform was seen as a way to give even more power to the *peninsulares*, who already controlled all of the important offices and were loyal to the Spanish throne.[9] All of these factors lit the revolutionary spark that already existed in New Spain and started a chain of events from 1808 to 1821 now known as the Mexican War of Independence.

The Mexican War of Independence

With the king gone, the Spanish started creating different juntas all throughout the nation, with each claiming that they should be in power instead of the new king. These juntas sent word to New Spain, asking them for support in their struggle for power. However, the instability and chaos that were created with the absence of a real king, as well as already existing internal problems, caused much confusion in the province. The viceroy of New Spain at the time, José de Iturrigaray, could not decide which junta to support, and the matter caused a great debate between the criollos, who were in favor of independence, and the *peninsulares*, who believed that New Spain was a colony and opposed the idea of self-governance. Afraid that they were going to lose the power that they held for years, the *peninsulares* staged a coup, deposing José de Iturrigaray and putting one of their own in power. With the power that they held and despite the instability that it had caused for almost two years, the *peninsulares* recognized the Junta of Aranjuez as legitimate and received a new viceroy in the form of Francisco Javier Venegas from mainland Spain.[10] The new viceroy landed in New Spain on September 14th, 1810. The very next day, with the command of a local priest and a

---

[9] Von Wobeser, Gisela. "La consolidación de vales reales como factor determinante de la lucha de independencia en México, 1804–1808." Historia mexicana (2006).

[10] David E. Narrett. (2012). "Geopolitics and Intrigue: James Wilkinson, the Spanish Borderlands, and Mexican Independence." The William and Mary Quarterly, 69(1), 101–146. https://doi.org/10.5309/willmaryquar.69.1.0101

criollo by the name of Miguel Hidalgo y Costilla, about six hundred men started marching south from the town of Dolores to Mexico City, seeking a revolution.

On September 15th, 1810, Hidalgo and his men started moving toward Mexico City. Hidalgo was a monarchist and still supported the legitimacy of the true king of Spain: Ferdinand VII. However, as thousands joined Hidalgo, one aspect became clear for the movement—to gain independence from Spain and end the rule of the *peninsulares*. By the time they reached Mexico City, the army consisted of almost 100,000 people. Almost none of them were professionally trained soldiers. Despite this, Hidalgo was able to defeat the forces of the viceroy outside Mexico City, but he decided not to proceed further and take the capital. Instead, his forces turned back to the city of Guadalajara. Hidalgo is still criticized for this move to this day since it enabled the Spanish forces to regroup and defeat his army at a bridge near the Calderón River.[11] This forced Hidalgo to flee to the north, probably in an attempt to seek support from the Americans, but he was chased down and arrested. He was placed on trial, and in the end, he was found guilty and executed on July 30th, 1811.

However, the revolutionary movement was still alive. José María Morelos was now leading the insurgence, and he had much clearer goals in mind when it came to the revolution. The main difference between the two was that Morelos was a *mestizo*, so he understood the racial discrimination and the struggles that came with being part of this class very well. Thus, he fought with much more pride and motivation.[12] His smaller but more disciplined army took control of the southern part of the country, and in 1813, he held the Congress of Chilpancingo, where he signed a declaration of independence in

---

[11] Guedea, Virginia. "The First Popular Elections in Mexico City, 1812–1813" in the Evolution of the Mexican Political System. Jaime E. Rodríguez O., ed. Wilmington: Scholarly Resources 1993.

[12] Guedea, (1993).

November of that same year. The document not only declared Mexico to be a free nation from Spain but also recognized Catholicism as its official religion and abolished slavery, putting an end to other types of racial discrimination in the country and shattering the social system that had been in place.

This was a pivotal point in Mexico's struggle for independence. Despite this, the Spanish, who were now under the rule of King Ferdinand VII, were ordered to crush the rebellion and put the revolutionaries back in their place. In 1815, the Spanish Army managed to capture and execute Morelos, destabilizing the region even more and starting a series of conflicts throughout the country that did not take an organized form until 1820.

The revolutionaries found their savior in Agustín de Iturbide. Even though he had previously served on the side of the Spanish and fought against the uprising, Iturbide and his army switched sides after negotiating a deal with the republican leader Vicente Guerrero. The two drafted the Plan of Iguala in 1821, borrowing from the previous declaration by Morelos and stating the "guarantees" of the nation were its independence, equality, and the prevalence of Catholicism. Then, with the Army of the Three Guarantees, they took Mexico City and forced the Spanish to sign the Treaty of Córdoba, finally ending the Spanish rule over New Spain and becoming the Mexican Empire. After thirteen years of struggle, Mexico was finally independent.

The Mexicans, just like other peoples of the 19th century, managed to free themselves from the colonial rule of the Europeans. In the wake of the new nation, the people's eyes were set upon their future, which promised to be full of surprises. But the following years were not exactly easy for an independent Mexico. Instead of relief, further instability and internal conflicts continued to plague the country. The social and political problems that were caused after Mexico's independence played a crucial part in the Mexican-American War. They provided a basis for the occurrence of significant events such as the Texas Revolution and were among the reasons for Mexico's defeat in the war.

Chapter 2 – The Struggles of the Mexican Republic and the Texas Revolution

Early Independence Years

Even though becoming independent was a major achievement for the Mexican people, it was ultimately gained by Agustín de Iturbide and Vicente Guerrero. It is imperative to remember that Iturbide was a general of the Spanish forces first, fighting to crush the rebellion, but that he switched sides and joined Guerrero's army. During the war, they were able to set aside their differences and, with the Army of the Three Guarantees—independence, equality, and religion—achieved victory. However, as Mexico began its existence as a republic, the conflicts between the two parties started coming back.

Since no European ruler wanted to become the emperor of Mexico, Iturbide was eventually proclaimed as the first emperor, becoming Agustín I.[13] However, his rule lasted for only about two years. Iturbide was not half as good of an administrator as he was a general, and Mexico could not work as a constitutional monarchy

---

[13] Russell, P. (2011). *The History of Mexico: From Pre-conquest to Present*. Routledge.

because of the harsh divides between the Mexican population. Of course, there were republicans who wanted the nation to become a democracy instead of a monarchy. They believed that the abolishment of the caste system was not supported by the emperor, but what's also interesting is that a large number of conservatives also disliked him as a ruler. Some of them, especially in the northern part of the country, were upset by the fact that the class system was no longer in place, and some believed that Mexico should have been ruled by a Spanish monarch, not a criollo. Both the far left and the far right hated him, and eventually, a rebellion, which was led by the republicans, forced him to abdicate in 1823.

This still did not solve Mexico's problems. After Iturbide's abdication, Mexico largely became a federalist country. The power of Mexico City was decentralized, and individual provinces were given the right to self-govern. This decision felt natural, organic, and legitimate for the Mexican people.[14] Despite this, Mexican national identity was still largely unknown, and it was not communicated well enough amongst the people, causing Central American provinces to peacefully secede from Mexico and become independent.[15] In addition, years of war had impacted the Mexican economy. The reserves were largely empty, and Mexico had accumulated severe debt from other nations, including the US, France, and Great Britain. Plus, industries like mining, which were the driving forces behind the economy, started declining due to the Spanish *peninsulares*. They backed these industries but were leaving the country for Europe. Not only that, but the country was still largely divided between the federalist republicans and the more conservative centralists. The best demonstration of this is the fact that after the election of the first president Guadalupe Victoria in 1824, who was a federalist, power

---

[14] Anna, T. E. (1996). "Inventing Mexico: Provincehood and Nationhood after Independence." Bulletin of Latin American Research, 15(1), 7–17. http://www.jstor.org/stable/3339401.

[15] Anna (1996).

changed hands time and time again between the two opposing parties until the mid-1930s.

The Rise of Santa Anna

A portrait of Santa Anna. (Source: Manuel Paris; Wikimedia Commons)

Antonio López de Santa Anna is considered by many to be the central figure in the early history of independent Mexico. He was a Mexican general who rose to power during the events that took place in the country after it gained independence, and he remained to dominate the scene in the following years. Santa Anna is a classic example of a *caudillo*—a charismatic, authoritative military leader who managed to gain power and influence politics through unconventional means.[16] At first, he fought alongside Iturbide for independence in 1821, but he became one of the leaders of the coup that deposed him and advocated for Mexico becoming a republic. Later on, he switched sides between the federalists and conservatives, favoring one over the other based on the political climate at that time. In short, Santa Anna was a cunning political figure who, over the years, slid in and out of the Mexican political scene and became a prominent actor in both the Texas Revolution and the Mexican-American War.

Santa Anna gained much of his popularity when he defeated the Spanish in their efforts to reconquer Mexico at the Battle of Tampico in 1829. Due to the fact that the Mexican government was predominantly federalist at that time, defeating the Spanish and driving the republic's oldest enemies out of the country was considered to be a massive achievement. For this reason, Santa Anna was chosen as the next president in 1833. However, he put the vice president, Valentín Gómez Farías, in charge and did not directly start to serve as the president until 1834. While the exact reason behind this is unknown, it is speculated that maybe he was waiting for the "right time" to make his appearance once again.[17]

This time came in May of 1834 when the Mexican population, especially the conservatives, were enraged by Farías's reforms, which stripped the Catholic Church of all its lands and reduced its role in education. This move was seen as anti-conservative, and it clearly was. Therefore, Santa Anna swept in and took the office from Farías. He dissolved Congress, organized a more centralist-conservative government, and gave the church much of its power back. He essentially took advantage of the political climate that favored him—an action that is typical of a *caudillo*.[18] Not only that, but in 1835, Santa

---

[16] Wolf, E. R., & Hansen, E. C. (1967). "Caudillo Politics: A Structural Analysis." Comparative Studies in Society and History, 9(2), 168–179. http://www.jstor.org/stable/177739.

[17] Krauze, E. (1997). *Mexico: Biography of Power* (p. 896). New York: HarperCollins.

[18] Fowler, W. (2007). *Santa Anna of Mexico*. University of Nebraska Press.

Anna introduced a new constitution called the "Seven Laws," which replaced the old one of 1824. This constitution further increased the central government's power. All of this led to mass discontent within some of the states of Mexico, most importantly in the state of Texas, which led to the Texas Revolution.

The Texas Revolution

The Texas Revolution was a turning point of the 19th-century history of both Mexico and the United States. It is considered to be one of the main causes of the Mexican-American War, and it was influenced by a decade of events that took place prior to the revolution.

Texas had been a disputed region since the early colonial days. It technically belonged to Spain at first, with many Americans claiming it to be a part of the US. This was largely due to the US filibuster missions, which were privately funded military expeditions that claimed unsettled foreign lands, as well as the over-exaggeration of the amount of territory that was part of the Louisiana Purchase of 1803.[19] The US and Spain managed to solve the dispute in 1819 when the US officially relinquished its claims on Texas, establishing the borders that would go on to be a part of the Mexican Republic. In addition, the attacks of Native American tribes from the north posed a serious problem to the region. Every raid was brutal, leaving the people devastated and causing the region to be sparsely populated.[20]

To put an end to this, the Mexican Republic decided to welcome Americans who wanted to settle in Texas by granting them a title of empresario.[21] In 1825, after receiving the title of empresario from his father, Stephen F. Austin managed to convince some three hundred

---

[19] Oxford English Dictionary. "Filibuster." Retrieved October 14, 2021.

[20] Rodriguez, S. K. M. (2017). "'The Greatest Nation on Earth': The Politics and Patriotism of the First Anglo American Immigrants to Mexican Texas, 1820–1824." Pacific Historical Review, 86(1), 50–83. https://www.jstor.org/stable/26419727.

[21] Rodriguez (2017).

US families to move and "colonize" the eastern part of the region. In the hopes of keeping the Native Americans, most notably the Comanche and the Apache tribes, out of the region, the settlers were provided with weapons to defend their property. Even though the influx of immigrants was seen as a success at first, it eventually did not stop the raids; it only displaced them farther northwest. Additional problems arose along the way, as most of the US families were slave-owners. They brought their slaves with them to Mexico, where the practice of slavery had been made illegal. Besides, the American empresarios were required by the government to convert to Catholicism and learn Spanish against their will, often causing them to not follow the rules. This, paired with the fact that, by the 1830s, the American empresario population vastly outnumbered the *Tejano* population of Mexican-born Texans, caused additional divisions in the region.[22] Furthermore, the Law of April 6, 1830, by the conservative Mexican government increased taxes, further enforced the ban on slavery, and did not allow for any new American settlers to come to Texas. However, settlers continued to immigrate to the area and simply ignored the newly introduced laws.Illegal immigration and societal disputes aside, Santa Anna and his reforms played a crucial role in the relations between Texas and Mexico.[23] At first, after his election as the president in 1833, Texans were given some power, as their representation in legislative matters was increased, but ultimately, Santa Anna dissolved Congress and pursued conservative policies, making pro-federalist Texas even more upset. During this period, fighting broke out in the central and southern provinces of Mexico, but the rebels were quickly crushed by Santa Anna's forces, which relentlessly dealt with everyone they captured.

---

[22] Rodriguez (2017).

[23] Shadle, Stan. "Review of The First Century of Mexican Independence, by Ward S. Albro, Leslie Bethell, Helen Delpar, Michael C. Meyer, William L. Sherman, Allen Peskin, Jasper Ridley, et al." Latin American Research Review 31, no. 1 (1996): 244–58. http://www.jstor.org/stable/2503860.

The final spark for a revolution was lit on September 10th, 1835, when a Mexican soldier who was stationed in Texas had a fight with a citizen in Gonzales. In fears of starting a conflict with an outraged populace that held the majority in the region, the Mexican commander in Texas sent a small force to retrieve the cannon that had been given to the settlers as a means of protection against Native American raids. The citizens quickly took up arms and defended the cannon, raising the famous flag that said "Come and take it."[24] The Mexican force, which was facing a disadvantage, ultimately retreated, bringing the first victory to the Texans. Even though no real fighting erupted (it was more of an inconsequential stand-off between the two sides), the news of the encounter quickly spread all over Texas, uniting the people and motivating them to fight against Mexican rule.[25] Not only that, but many volunteers also joined the revolution directly from the US by crossing the border, even though the Andrew Jackson administration did not directly contribute any aid to the rebellion.

A reproduction of the "come and take it" flag. (Source: Daniel Mayer; Wikimedia Commons)

[24] Bennet, M. S. (1899). "The Battle of Gonzales, the 'Lexington' of the Texas Revolution." The Quarterly of the Texas State Historical Association, 2(4), 313–316. http://www.jstor.org/stable/30242776.

[25] Davis, W. C. (2017). *Lone Star Rising*. Simon and Schuster.

The mobilization of the citizens all throughout Texas eventually forced the Mexican Army out of the region, and they established a provisional government in its place called the Consultation. The Consultation met in November to discuss and clarify the reasons behind the fighting. During the convention, they elected Sam Houston as the leader of the army and established that they would not rejoin Mexico until the Constitution of 1824 was reinstituted and the federalist government held power in Mexico City. However, the members of the Consultation were still largely divided within their own ranks, with a portion of them advocating for declaring independence. Ultimately, the convention did not declare independence in November, but this opposition of views would cause major problems later on.

Santa Anna quickly reacted to the uprising and decided to address the issue personally. He assembled an army of about six thousand troops and embarked on an expedition toward Texas in December of 1835. They believed that the rebellion would be easy to defeat.[26] In addition, Santa Anna's government passed the Tornel Decree, which was a clear articulation of the conservatives' anti-American sentiment. It stated that everyone who fought against Mexico were to be treated as pirates and permitted the Mexican Army to execute all prisoners of war immediately.[27] On February 23rd, 1836, Santa Anna's forces reached the small fort of the Alamo, which had been captured by the Texans. Alamo was not a strong fortification, as it had been built mainly to withstand Native American attacks, making it unfit for cannon fire.[28] However, Santa Anna's progress was halted for about two weeks at the Alamo because of the Texans' relentless fighting.

[26] Davis (2017).

[27] Haynes, S.W., Saxon, G.D., Cantrell, G., Schlereth, E., Haynes, S.W., & Soto, M. (2015). *Contested Empire: Rethinking the Texas Revolution*. College Station: Texas A&M University Press.

[28] Jeffries, C. (1942). "The Lights of the Alamo." The Southwestern Historical Quarterly, 46(1), 1–8. http://www.jstor.org/stable/30240588.

Even though the garrison had received some minor reinforcements, Santa Anna's troops were able to finally take the fort on March 6th, losing between five hundred and six hundred men in the process.

Although the Alamo was an insignificant military accomplishment for the Mexicans, it had a huge impact on the Texans. The garrison managed to hold off the Mexican advance and bought time for the Texans to regroup. It was also a huge motivating factor for them in the future, especially in the Battle of San Jacinto. It also allowed the Consultation to meet on March 1st in Washington-on-the-Brazos, where they agreed on declaring independence from Mexico. The Constitution of the Republic of Texas was prepared and presented. It borrowed heavily from the US Constitution and made it clear that the reason behind their secession was the violation of the Mexican Constitution of 1824 and the tyranny of Santa Anna's regime.[29]

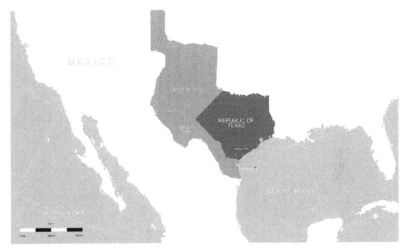

The darker area was the Republic of Texas, while the lighter green is merely territory that the republic claimed but had no ownership of. (Source: Wikimedia Commons)

After the Alamo, Santa Anna was confident in his victory and marched on Goliad, where he continued his no-prisoner policy, executing up to 350 men after a week of skirmishes. The Alamo and

---

[29] Jeffries (1942).

Goliad once again showed the Texans the relentless nature of Santa Anna. It also gave them a further motivating factor of vengeance for their fallen. They managed to avenge their fallen brothers at the decisive Battle of San Jacinto, where about 900 Texans managed to defeat an army of about 1,300 Mexicans. It was then that the famous phrase of "Remember the Alamo" was first born, with the words being shouted by enraged Texans as they thundered across the battlefield. This battle ended in a victory for Texas, which was led by Houston. The Texans only suffered around fifteen casualties, while the Mexicans fared much worse. About six hundred lay dead on the field, and about seven hundred were captured, including Santa Anna himself.[30]

Even though many soldiers wanted to execute Santa Anna for the crimes that he had committed against the Texan people, he was ultimately spared. After weeks of negotiations, he was finally set free on June 1st, 1836. According to the Treaties of Velasco, which were signed by Santa Anna, Mexico would remove all troops south of the Rio Grande River, establishing a new unofficial border with Texas. In private, Santa Anna also promised to lobby the Mexican government to officially recognize the independence of Texas once he safely got back to Mexico City.

The Effects of the War

The Texas Revolution was one of the few successful rebellions against centralist-conservative Mexico. With its secession, Mexico spun into yet another period of instability, even though it never actually recognized the independence of Texas. Santa Anna returned to the country, defeated for the first time. The revolution had turned out to be too much to surmount, even for a powerful *caudillo*. Mexico's budget was completely depleted, and the successful secession of Texas caused even more pro-federalist movements

---

[30] Winters, J. W. (1902). "An Account of the Battle of San Jacinto." The Quarterly of the Texas State Historical Association, 6(2), 139–144. http://www.jstor.org/stable/27784928.

throughout the country, which aimed to follow in its footsteps. The southern neighbors of Texas unified in 1840 under the proclaimed name of the Republic of the Rio Grande. The raids of the Comanche resumed after the revolution as well, with even more devastating effects along the Rio Grande. For years, the centralist Mexican government used the war with Texas as an excuse to increase taxation and the army's funding in the hopes of reconquering the lands that they had lost.

Tensions increased between Mexico and the United States as well. Mexico believed that Texas managed to win the war only due to the help received from the US, even though the United States was never directly involved in the conflict. However, it is true that a significant portion of the Texan army included American volunteers, some of them even members of the US Army. The US, on the other hand, recognized independent Texas in 1837. At that time, the United States' expansionist policy of Manifest Destiny was starting to come into fruition, and many Americans were in favor of the annexation of Texas.[31] The harsh political climate between the two countries continued in the 1840s and ultimately caused the Mexican-American War, with a recently defeated Mexico trying to maintain its power on one side and a powerful expansionist US on the other.

---

[31] Diaz, M. A. (2016). "To Conquer the Coast: Pensacola, the Gulf of Mexico, and the Construction of American Imperialism, 1820-1848." The Florida Historical Quarterly, 95(1), 1–25. http://www.jstor.org/stable/24769295.

Chapter 3 – Manifest Destiny and the Pre-War United States

Foreign Policy in the Early 19ᵗʰ-Century US

Now that we have covered the sociopolitical developments in Mexico, we need to also take a look at what was happening in parallel to Mexico's events on the other side of the border in the young but already well-established nation of the United States of America. The matters in the early 19ᵗʰ-century US played a huge role in the war between the two nations. Understanding pre-war United States in its entirety is a challenging matter in itself. However, let's dive deep into one of the most interesting albeit less well-known periods in US history, starting with probably the most influential secretary of state of all time, John Quincy Adams, and US foreign policy in the early 19ᵗʰ century.

In 1812, after decades of tense relations and disputes with Great Britain, the two countries went to war. However, the war turned out to be relatively unsuccessful for both sides. In 1814, after the Treaty of Ghent, both Great Britain and the US agreed on establishing the pre-war borders, restoring their relations. Even though it was ultimately an inconsequential war, it would become one of the factors upon which the Americans would base their foreign policy. After the end of the war, British ships were free to safely transport British goods and carry out naval trade. Because American merchants at the time were akin to carrying and transporting goods, not only US products but also anyone's goods, the US traders had to find more profitable jobs, which they found in the ever-growing local US industry.[32] Despite this, however, not all were able to overcome the economic difficulties caused by the war, and they were motivated to start moving westward and explore the sparsely populated lands to find their fortune. This led to the creation of more and more American settlements outside of the original US states in places as far west as Oregon and California.

The diplomatic genius of Secretary of State John Quincy Adams made the American people realize that they were strong enough to challenge the domination of European powers. Adams understood that Britain, despite the fact that it could not decisively defeat the United States in 1812, still potentially posed the biggest threat to the American people. Britain occupied Canada and controlled the seas, and if the British were not kept at bay, Americans would not be free to carry out their internal affairs in peace, which, Adams believed, were also linked with further expansion. However, where Adams showed his brilliancy was that he understood that the British also wanted to weaken Spanish power in the Americas. This was due to the fact that Britain would be able to develop its markets and gain massive profits from the newly established Latin American republics. The US also wanted Spain out of the continent, as it desired Florida as both a valuable and a strategic territory.[33] It also considered Spain to be a potential rival in establishing new settlements in the unexplored areas of the continent. Therefore, Adams got to work.

Adams was able to negotiate with the British at the Convention of 1818, which was a historic pact that established the border between the Canadian territory and the US along the forty-ninth parallel. It also

---

[32] LaFeber, W. (1994). *The American Age: United States Foreign Policy at Home and Abroad since 1750* (2nd ed.). Norton. pp.71-72.

[33] Diaz (2016).

softened trade regulations and granted both countries joint control over the Oregon Territory for the next ten years.[34] This contained the British in the north, so Adams then turned to the Spanish and started negotiations over Florida. As we already know, Spain was struggling in the 1810s, trying to hold onto its holdings in the New World because of instability caused by Napoleon in Iberia. The Spanish minister to Washington at the time, Luis de Onís y González, tried stalling the talks for as long as he could. Adams even admitted the diplomat's unmatched resilience himself, claiming to have never met anyone "as much of a swindler as he was."[35]

The tensions hit the roof when President James Monroe ordered General Andrew Jackson to contain the Native American attacks coming from Florida at the US border. However, the latter, instead of just being defensively stationed at the border, marched into eastern Florida and destroyed the Seminole villages, executing two British citizens and claiming the region for his nation in the process. This caused much uproar in the Monroe cabinet, which seriously considered denouncing the actions of Jackson. However, Adams defended Jackson, saying that the two British citizens who were killed were in the wrong and blamed them for motivating the Native American tribes for their attacks on the Americans. This managed to gain the support of the cabinet and pushed the negotiations over Florida with Luis de Onís. In the end, the two parties agreed to the Transcontinental Treaty, with Florida becoming part of the US and Spain giving up its claims on Oregon. The United States, on the other hand, agreed to recognize the borders of Spain, which included Texas (Adams was personally against this point, but he was overruled by President Monroe).[36]

---

[35] LaFeber (1994), p. 78.

[36] Britannica, T. Editors of Encyclopedia (2019, October 21). "Transcontinental Treaty." Encyclopedia Britannica. https://www.britannica.com/event/Transcontinental-Treaty

These two victories, which were achieved by Adams in the span of just three years, indicated a promising future for the country. The expansionist mindset was already well-rooted in the minds of Americans, and even though they were relatively new to the concept, at least in comparison to their British or Spanish neighbors, the US was successfully pursuing it. However, to further pursue its goals, it was becoming more and more apparent that the country had to confront the internal problems that came with expansion, most importantly the issue of slavery.

The Slavery Divide

By the 19th century, the United States was heavily divided on the matter of slavery. Slavery had been legal in the Thirteen Colonies, for the most part, since the early 1600s, but with the US gaining independence, abolitionist movements started popping up throughout the country by the mid-18th century. Over the years, these movements gained more and more traction, with enslaved black populations collecting and sending petitions to local legislative organs. By 1789, the states of Pennsylvania, New Hampshire, Massachusetts, Rhode Island, and Connecticut had declared the full or partial abolition of slavery in their states, while the eight remaining states still continued the practice. At the Constitutional Convention of 1789, where the new constitution was to be drafted, the matter of slavery was addressed and greatly debated. The issue was never directly mentioned in the Constitution, but it was definitely acknowledged in the meetings. With the expanding US and the creation of more and more states, the tendency of Northern states being abolitionist and Southern states being pro-slavery began to emerge. The superficial divides like the Mason-Dixon Line and the Ohio River became boundaries of where one could or could not practice slavery. And to keep the balance, there had to be an equal number of slave and free states.

This system was weak, to say the least, mainly because of the sketchy geographical divide and legal ambiguity. The unofficial divide affected practically everything, especially the economic systems of the two parts of the country. In the North, a free-labor market emerged with an industrial and commercial complex; in the South, a slave-centered agricultural system became the most prominent. Foreign policy practices were also influenced by the internal struggles and vice versa, as whatever efforts were made in the international scene had their own consequences domestically.[37] Political actors naturally formed their personalities based on where they came from too. John Quincy Adams, for example, was a Northerner; therefore, he was very much against slavery and tried to implement his views in his policies.

Crucially, in 1819, Missouri applied as a slave state. It had been a part of the territories acquired in the Louisiana Purchase of 1803, and the Northern states proposed that slavery would be declared illegal in any states formed out of the Louisiana Territory, which still included a huge area in the central part of the country. The South, of course, denied the proposal, the reason being that the territory promised to be a further expansion point where slavery could be practiced. The debate raged on, with neither side being able to come to terms with the other.

Adams paid attention to the developments with great care. He firmly believed that a divide of this magnitude would greatly affect its efforts to continue expansion westward. He understood that American expansion could no longer be discussed without having to decide whether slave or free states would benefit from this growth, calling the Missouri debate "a mere preamble – a title-page to a great tragic volume."[38] He did not want to acquire any new territory, especially if it included war and the loss of American lives, for it to be then used by Southern states to practice slavery. With all these concerns, the Missouri Compromise in 1820 established Missouri as a slave state and also introduced Maine as a free state, keeping the balance between the two. In addition, it agreed that the future territory of

---

[37] LaFeber (1994), pp. 81-82.

[38] LaFeber (1994), p. 82.

Louisiana would be divided, with slavery prohibited in the Northern states but allowed in the Southern ones.

Adams did not believe that the compromise would solve the problem, and he was right. Even though the Missouri Compromise was at first seen as a democratic achievement, what it also did was divide the country even more. As the United States continued to expand, the matter of slavery continued to play a big role in the determination of its policies. This especially became apparent when it came to the annexation of Texas, which ultimately caused the Mexican-American War and later the Civil War.

The Monroe Doctrine

Despite the ever-so-apparent internal divide that was brewing inside the US, the country continued to excel economically and continued its expansionist efforts. A critical development would occur on December 2nd, 1823, during President James Monroe's address to Congress. The president would go on to state what is now referred to as the "Monroe Doctrine," summarizing the country's foreign policy achievements with the introduction of a set of principles. These principles were largely influenced by Adams, who was still a major actor in Monroe's cabinet. His firm belief in the United States' destiny to take control of the whole continent and drive out its enemies, most notably the Europeans and Native Americans, greatly shaped the Monroe Doctrine. Adams believed that it was only natural that America belonged to the American people, calling the continent of North America their "proper dominion."[39] Adams was convinced that, sooner or later, people living on the continent would ultimately become a part of the United States, one way or another. In his eyes, this was inevitable, and he believed that everyone who lived in the country needed to be familiar with the concept. To a large degree, a lot of Americans did agree. However, Adams was the one who

---

[39] Paterson, T. G. (2005). Major Problems in American Foreign Relations: Documents and Essays. (D. Merrill, Ed.) (Sixth, Ser. Major problems in American history series). Houghton Mifflin. P. 147.

publicly advocated for his beliefs. As we will see later on, Adams's ideas would thrive even after he was not as much of a prominent political figure.

The Monroe Doctrine was also greatly inspired by the events that took place at the beginning of 1823. With the acquisition of Florida and the fast-paced expansion of the US in the West, it was apparent to the European powers that the United States was becoming a force to be reckoned with. The way Adams and many Americans thought of the continent as belonging solely to them presented the United States as both ambitious and aggressive, and the Europeans tried everything to hold onto the influence they had in the region. As previously mentioned, the best example of this was Britain's efforts of gaining access to the rapidly developing markets of Latin America. When an economic power vacuum was left in the region due to the series of revolutions, Britain tried asserting its economic dominance and was against the reestablishment of Spanish colonies, even though it never got involved militarily. Britain also wanted the US to formally join them in keeping the other European powers, most notably Spain, out of the region, by publicly declaring that the country would support the development of newly born nations in South America and pledging that the two powers would not aim at gaining control over the territories themselves.

The new British foreign secretary, George Canning, officially approached the US with the proposal. President Monroe consulted former US Presidents James Madison and Thomas Jefferson on the matter, with both presidents recommending accepting Canning's offer.[40] However, John Quincy Adams opposed it. He was as wary of the British as ever, and he convinced Monroe to retain freedom from them. Adams believed that aligning with the British would pose a problem to the United States in its imminent future expansion, especially with territories like Texas and Cuba. Therefore, when President Monroe addressed the Union with his speech in December

---

[40] Paterson (2005), p. 148.

of 1823, he made sure to clarify the position of the American nation, which was inspired by the reasoning provided by Adams.

The main principle of the Monroe Doctrine was declaring a strong position against future colonization of the New World by any European power. The United States wanted no further direct intervention of the Europeans in matters that occurred in the Americas. Monroe stated the American continents belonged to its inhabitants, not to anyone else, and especially not to the Europeans seeking to regain much of the control that they had lost over the years. Monroe emphasized that any intervention by a European power would be considered "as dangerous to [American people's] peace and safety."[41] As historian William E. Weeks puts it, "In effect, Monroe had defined the American security zone to include the entire Western Hemisphere. A justification was in place for the future US interventions throughout Latin America."[42] The United States had declared itself, somewhat boldly, to be a "protector" of the free nations of the New World that were gaining their liberty from European rule. However, this went both ways, meaning that the United States would not interfere with matters in Europe. This included both direct wars and internal affairs that existed within Europe.[43]

The Monroe Doctrine was one of the pivotal moments in 19th-century US history. The newly established South American republics thought of it as America's wish of organizing a potential all-American alliance. This was never the intention of Monroe and Adams, however, and even though they recognized the independence movements, they never officially agreed to make their policy multilateral. Not only that, but European countries like Russia were affected too. Tsar Alexander I of Russia had declared claims on all

[41] Paterson (2005), p. 149.

[42] Paterson (2005), p. 149.

[43]Britannica, T. Editors of Encyclopedia (2021, August 18). "Monroe Doctrine." Encyclopedia Britannica. https://www.britannica.com/event/Monroe-Doctrine

lands north of the fifty-first parallel in North America, including parts of Oregon, Alaska, and the Aleutian Islands. Plus, no non-Russian ships were to be allowed within one hundred miles of their coasts, causing discontent among American merchants. But after the strong anti-European message asserted by the Monroe Doctrine, paired with the financial problems that came with the prohibition of American merchants to trade in the abovementioned lands, the tsar was forced to take back his claims and let American ships have access to the northwestern coast. The United States was incentivized to uphold its two-spheres policy too. Back in 1821, it did not involve itself in the Greek uprising against Turkish rule, despite the popularity of Greece and the Greek culture among many Americans, especially young students.[44] The US neutrality in the Greek crisis was supported by and explained the essence of the Monroe Doctrine's two-spheres policy.

The Monroe Doctrine was a culmination of the foreign policy the US had pursued since the mid-1810s. In a way, it was also a celebration of its accomplishments. After all, in just a span of two decades, the United States was able to gain a huge amount of territory in the form of the Louisiana Purchase, stabilize its relations with Great Britain, and acquire Florida from the Spanish and further weaken its position on the continent (which eventually helped cause the Mexican Revolution). The nation established its claims on the rest of the disputed lands of the region (mainly Oregon) and managed to develop a thriving economy that included both a dominant free-labor market and industrial complex, as well as a developed agricultural sector, all while keeping external threats mostly at bay. What was left for the American people? What other ambitions did they have? The answer was simple—they needed to realize their goals that were divine in nature. They needed to manifest their destiny.

---

[44] LaFeber (1994), p. 86.

American Progress *by John Gast. The women pictured is Columbia, and she is leading the people westward. (Source: Wikimedia Commons)*

The Age of Manifest Destiny

The late 1820s and 1830s saw a relative halt when it came to the expansionist efforts on the western front. During this period, the United States was not able to acquire a significant amount of territory, despite the fact that the Monroe Doctrine presented the pinnacle of American expansionist ideals. Instead, the country focused more on increasing its power indirectly, mostly through economic means. It was during these years that more and more Americans started emigrating into Texas. The United States also established trade with distant partners such as China, allowing it to gain much control on the Pacific trade routes. Most importantly, however, it was the internal political divide within the country and the ideological differences that came with it that haltered US expansion.

While John Quincy Adams's efforts as secretary of state remain one of the most successful and influential to this day, his presidency years, which lasted from 1825 to 1829, were not nearly as effective as one might think. During his presidency, Adams unsuccessfully tried to pursue his expansionist ideas by failing to acquire Texas, which, at that time, was still a part of the newly independent Mexico. He also renewed the pact with Britain about co-governing Oregon, which is often referred to as his greatest achievement as president. However, he was defeated by Andrew Jackson in the 1828 elections, and a new era of American politics began.

The political climate of the United States in the 1820s and 1830s was dominated by the two most prominent political parties: the Whigs and the Democrats. The Whig Party was, for the most part, opposed to direct land expansion, favoring a more mercantile process. The party mostly included wealthier, often slave-owning members like Henry Clay. It stood for the development of the internal American market, which would affect the commercial and manufacturing sectors. The Democrats, on the other hand, were all about expansion. Notable Democrats, like Jackson himself and Polk, who was the president during the war with Mexico, were notorious expansionists. The Democratic Party favored the decentralization of the government, which would leave the states' individual legislatures holding more power. This division in the country meant that the elections were more and more focused on the presidency. The winner would be able to virtually control Congress and stand basically unopposed when it came to proposing new policies, especially ones concerning foreign affairs.[45]

It was not until the mid-1840s that the term "Manifest Destiny" entered the scene of US politics. Novel in name but not in its nature, the term described the divine right of the United States to expand. However, the exact area of expansion was not defined. Did the people envision expanding westward to the Pacific? Did it mean dominating the continent by gaining control over Canada and Mexico? Was it so ambitious as to mean the whole hemisphere? Despite this ambiguity, it appealed to the public. Manifest Destiny was far more idealistic than the previous expansionist thoughts. It was a mission, endowed by

---

[45] LaFeber (1994), p. 97.

heaven, to spread the American ideals of freedom and democracy. It might take years, decades, even centuries to fulfill this destiny, but it was the duty of the American people. Everyone who wished to become a part of the temple of freedom was to be admitted. For some, like the Mexicans, it would be a more gradual process, taking much more time and effort to "convert" them to the American way, but to the American people, it was inevitable.[46]

It was John O'Sullivan—the editor of the *Democratic Review* and a visionary, literary artist, scholar, adventurer, and politician—that first coined the term in December of 1845.[47] He was a firm believer that God had blessed the United States:

"The last order of civilization, which is democratic, received its first permanent existence in this country...A land separated from the influences of ancient arrangement, peculiar in its position, productions, and extent, wide enough to hold a numerous people, admitting with facility, intercommunication and trade, vigorous and *fresh from the hand of God*, was requisite for the full and broad manifestation of the free spirit of the new-born democracy." [Italics added][48]

Spreading America's ideas of freedom and democracy did not only mean political democracy and equality. It also meant economic democracy. With increasing immigration from Ireland and Germany, Americans were becoming more and more aware of the troubles economic instability could cause. Many saw the freedom of land ownership and the ease of land acquisition as their divine right, as something that all people should be able to experience. For many, the famine and poverty in Europe were caused by the exclusion and denial of this right. The realization of the "gifts of nature," or the

---

[46] Merk, F., & Merk, L. B. (1995). *Manifest Destiny and Mission in American History: A Reinterpretation* (1st Harvard University Press paperback). Harvard University Press. Pp. 24-25.

[47] Merk (1995), p. 27.

[48] Paterson (2005), p. 207.

natural resources on the lands occupied by the American people, was also one of the missions of Manifest Destiny. The United States clearly identified Mexico's failure to improve the rich lands of Texas and California, which seemed to have great potential. If these lands had been American, they would have been developed properly to fit the developed people who would live there. This would have been good for not only the American people but also other nations. They could all learn a valuable lesson of treating their natural "blessings" with respect.[49]

Another prevalent concept of Manifest Destiny was the United States' duty to "help" the underdeveloped peoples of the continent. Many Americans never truly believed that the Native Americans were capable of becoming full-fledged members of their society. President Jackson, most notably, declared in 1830, "What good man would prefer a country covered with forests and ranged by a few thousand savages to our extensive Republic, studded with cities, towns, and prosperous farms...occupied by more than 12,000,000 happy people, and filled with all the blessings of liberty, civilization, and religion?"[50]

During the late 1820s and 1830s, Native American tribes were forced to move westward, settling in what would become Oklahoma, which is north of Texas. Some tribes moved peacefully from their lands, while others resisted and were forced out, most notably the Seminoles and the Cherokees. The forceful removal of the Native Americans cost many lives. With the Native American population decimated, chased away miles from their homes, the Americans rejoiced in victory, having claimed their uncivilized and undeveloped lands for themselves.[51]

Technological advancements of the time also helped spread the idea of Manifest Destiny. By the 1840s, the introduction and

---

[49] Merk (1995), pp. 30-31.

[50] LaFeber (1994), p. 99.

[51] LaFeber (1994), p 100.

development of the steam engine proved to be crucial. The idea of building a transcontinental railroad that stretched from the East to the West, connecting the two oceans, became more and more prevalent. It would stand as a major feat of American engineering, something that would be seen as a clear, modern example of colonization and expansion. And what other country to set the course of embracing such ambitious projects than the glorious United States, which was destined to be the main locomotive of democracy and liberty in the region. In addition, developments in the communication field, most notably the telegraph, also set high hopes for the Americans. With it, the flow of information was made easier. The new opportunities that presented themselves with these advancements in technology were perfectly aligned with the expansionist ideas of the US.[52]

Now, not only would the American people be able to spread democracy and peace in the region, but they also modernized it by bringing these new technological feats with them, things never even dreamed of by the Native Americans and things that were far from being achieved properly in Mexico. Thus, the spread of Manifest Destiny propaganda was as prevalent as ever. The imagery of the time is a clear example. There are a lot of instances where the Native Americans appear to be defeated by what are effectively US soldiers and colonizers. In other cases, the colonizers, led by a white female figure dressed in white clothes, embodying the glory and the divine nature of the United States, are moving from the East to the West, driving the encountering herds of bison and groups of Native Americans away and claiming the lands for themselves.[53] These images reinforced pro-Manifest Destiny sentiments. They further served for the spread of ideas that those lands belonged to the United States by divine right.

---

[52] Merk (1995), pp. 50-51.

[53] Baigell, M. (1990). "Territory, Race, Religion: Images of Manifest Destiny." Smithsonian Studies in American Art, 4(3/4), 3–21. http://www.jstor.org/stable/3109013.

Manifest Destiny marked the return of expansionist US policies after a seemingly twenty-year break. Despite the fact that the period from 1823 to 1845 was relatively quieter when it came to direct expansion, the developments in the internal sociopolitical and economic landscapes directly contributed to bringing back that expansionist sentiment. Ironically, what President Monroe asserted in his address in 1823 had partially manifested itself during the period leading to the Mexican-American War. The US, which once had strong anti-colonist views, had become and even viewed itself as a proud colonizer. It believed that unlike the Europeans, who were only self-motivated, gluttonous conquerors who wanted to get a hold of the riches of the New World by exploiting the peoples of the Americas, it was destined to spread its ideals of democracy and liberty. The motivation behind the country's expansion was divine, as it had been given to the US by God himself, and no one was to stand in the way of its realization. Therefore, as we will see later on when it came to disputed matters like Texas and Oregon in the early 1840s and then the war with Mexico later in the decade, the United States had already established and justified its position. It thought of expansion as being divine in nature, something the American people had been destined to accomplish.

Chapter 4 – The Annexation of Texas

Post-Texas Revolution Mexico

In the previous chapter, we looked at the foreign and domestic policies of the 19th-century United States that are crucial to understanding the causes of the Mexican-American War. For now, let's take a break from the developments in the expansionist US policies and instead look at post-Texas-Revolution-Mexico.

After Mexico's loss in April of 1836 in the war with Texas, Santa Anna's reputation was in tatters. Despite the fact that he had been a renowned general, he could not manage to defend the rebellion due to his arrogance and underestimation of the Texans' spirit. As we already established, after Santa Anna was captured by the Texans at the end of the war, he agreed to two treaties in exchange for his freedom. The first one was public and asserted that all Mexican troops would retreat south of the Rio Grande River immediately. They would also not take up arms against the Texan forces anymore. According to the second treaty, which Santa Anna agreed to in secret, upon his return to Mexico, he would vouch for the independence of Texas and try to persuade the Mexican government to recognize it formally.

Back home, he found his name in disgrace. In 1837, General Anastasio Bustamante y Oseguera became the new president, with this government, of course, refuting any treaties that Santa Anna had made with Texas. He would not recognize Texas's independence. The ideas of reconquering the territory and asserting firm Mexican rule were also present amongst the people, but due to already existing internal struggles, no effort was made immediately.[54] At first, Santa Anna tried to win back public opinion by agreeing with the new government and also insisting that the promises he had made should not be honored since he was a prisoner of war at the time.[55] However, to avoid more backlash, he retired from political activities. He had worked on his reputation for more than a decade, dedicating his life to the Mexican people's best interests, or at least that was what he believed. Santa Anna was sure that, sooner or later, Mexico would need him once again, and as it turned out, he was right.

Santa Anna would redeem himself in the eyes of the Mexican people about a year later. In 1838, a growing number of French businessmen in Mexico complained about the Mexican government, demanding compensation for property damage caused by years of increasing civil unrest in the country. One of these Frenchmen was an owner of a pastry shop, and his store had been damaged time and time again by the Mexican military on different occasions. When the Mexican government refused to meet these claims, the French king, Louis Philippe, sent a naval force, blockading the port of Veracruz in April of 1838, a conflict that is now referred to as the Pastry War.[56] The French demanded an enormous amount of 600,000 pesos, which was ultimately agreed by the Mexican government in October. But by that time, the French demanded an additional 200,000 pesos—the cost of the blockade. Mexico would not pay that amount, so when the

---

[54] Miller, R. R. (1996). *Mexico: A History*. University of Oklahoma Press. P. 214.

[55] Suchlicki, J. (1996). *Mexico: From Montezuma to NAFTA, Chiapas, and Beyond.* Brassey's. P. 68.

[56] Suchlicki (1996), p. 68.

French ships started blockading the whole eastern Mexican coast and bombarded Veracruz, Mexico needed to act.[57]

Santa Anna would lead the Mexicans in this short war against the French. In typical *caudillo* fashion, he came out of retirement and offered his services to the government. The Mexican military at the time was not at its best, to say the least. Reorganization and mobilization of all forces were necessary, and only an experienced and charismatic leader such as Santa Anna would be able to do this. Thus, he personally commanded the troops in Veracruz, gaining a victory against about three thousand French soldiers who tried taking Veracruz in December. Famously, Santa Anna was wounded in the leg during the conflict and had it amputated, replacing it with a peg-leg that further strengthened his image as a distinct war hero and an accomplished veteran. He embraced this image with all his *caudillo* might, first burying the leg at his home estate but later disinterring it and dedicating it in a separate place at a national cemetery.[58] The Pastry War saw a swift and successful return of Santa Anna, who displayed his importance in Mexican politics once again.

The period from 1839 to 1846 (the outbreak of the Mexican-American War) is characterized by a number of internal revolts and transfers of power, much like most of the history of independent Mexico. An emerging characteristic of these revolts is the instance of one general overthrowing the other. Historians refer to these revolts as *cuartelazos*, or "barracks revolts."[59] After the victory in the Pastry War, Santa Anna was made an interim president for a short period of time while Bustamante was away fighting some federalist *cuartelazo* rebels. After Bustamante's return to Mexico City, Santa Anna went back to

---

[57] Miller (1996), p. 215.

[58] Suchlicki (1996), p. 69.

[59] "Cuartelazo." Encyclopedia of Latin American History and Culture. Retrieved October 27, 2021 from Encyclopedia.com: https://www.encyclopedia.com/humanities/encyclopedias-almanacs-transcripts-and-maps/cuartelazo

his private holdings, awaiting a favorable time to make his grand entrance.[60] The state of Yucatán, which was inspired by Texas, declared its independence in 1839 and struggled for the next four years to maintain it. Thus, stimulated by an increase in tariffs caused by a failing economy, further internal instability, and public discontent, Mexico was "ripe for another revolution."[61]

With all these existing problems, the Mexican sentiment of reconquering Texas and Yucatán was growing. Winning a war and recapturing the lost territories might have been the change the Mexican people needed to overcome the difficult situation that existed in the country. Mexico still had not recognized the independence of Texas, and it refused to do so, believing that it was just another albeit a bit more "serious" rebellion, which would be taken care of soon enough. So, in the midst of another military uprising in 1841, Santa Anna swept in as the provisional president, ultimately transforming the country into another dictatorship for three years.[62]

Santa Anna deeply wished to take back Texas. After all, the Texas Revolution was his first major defeat, and even though the victory in the Pastry War helped him gain back some respect, reconquering what he had personally lost would truly redeem him in the eyes of the Mexican people. The main problem he had to face, though, was an empty treasury. Years of consecutive warfare had depleted the reserves. The country was forced to take out foreign and domestic loans, which were not enough.[63] Therefore, Santa Anna turned to the church to provide the necessary funds for the war. Several new versions of the constitution were drafted, which showed centralist-conservative tendencies by referring to the territories as departments

---

[60] Bethell, L. (1991). *Mexico since Independence (The Cambridge History of Latin America)*. Cambridge University Press. P. 16.

[61] Bethell (1991), p. 17.

[62] Miller (1996), p. 216.

[63] Miller (1996), p. 216.

(rather than states). It also made Catholicism the sole religion of the country once again and enhanced the president's powers.[64]

With his official comeback at the head of Mexican politics, Santa Anna ordered his armies to carry out raids on Texas. While the Mexicans saw initial success in capturing San Antonio, the Texans, under the leadership of Sam Houston, responded, bouncing back and driving the Mexican troops out. Santa Anna was devastated. This defeat was a humiliation. Had the campaign been successful, he might have had the chance of consolidating his power and gaining public support, which he so desperately needed to stabilize the country. However, the reality was that Mexico was never truly capable of taking back Texas. Even other nations like Great Britain, which recognized the independence of Texas, encouraged Mexico to give up on its hopes of reconquering the lost territory and focus on its internal stability.[65] So, infuriated by the defeat, Mexico underwent yet another revolt, deposing and forcing Santa Anna into exile for life in 1844.

His replacement was General José Joaquín de Herrera. When France and Britain arranged the truce negotiations between Texas and Mexico, Herrera's government still refused to recognize Texas's independence. The resentment toward the Texans grew even more, which was stimulated by the fact that the United States was, in parallel, considering annexing the territory. Insisting that Texas was still a part of Mexico, the Mexican government declared that its annexation would be a declaration of war.[66] Herrera would not last too long as the president, though, as General Mariano Paredes rebelled against him in December 1845 and forced him to resign in January of the following year.

Ever since its independence, Mexico had been plagued by internal power struggles between different groups. After the Texas Revolution,

---

[64] Bethell (1991), pp. 17-19.

[65] Suchlicki (1996), p. 72.

[66] Bethell (1991), p. 19.

it was essentially a failed state, with a nonexistent economy, weak military, and mass corruption. All the different rulers during this period were busy bickering with each other over their ideological differences. They lusted for power, not taking the welfare of their people into consideration. The failed attempt to reconquer Texas boosted anti-American sentiment to its height. The Mexican government was desperate to take back its former territory, and after the election of the expansionist President James K. Polk in the US, the tense Mexican-American relations resulted in a war over the annexation of Texas.

Polk

Photograph of Polk (Source: Wikimedia Commons)

James K. Polk was elected as the president of the United States in 1844 after being considered a "dark horse" candidate by many.[67] In the elections, he managed to defeat both leading candidates, the Democrat Martin Van Buren and the Whig Henry Clay. Unlike these

---

[67] LaFeber (1994), p. 107.

two, who favored mercantile expansion and focused on internal issues like tariffs, Polk publicly advocated for the annexation of Texas and the "reoccupation of Oregon." This became a major factor in his successful campaign, enabling Polk to win by a thin margin. However, when he stepped into office, he had to deal with crises on two fronts. First, he had to strike a new deal with the British about the matters in Oregon; then, he had to address the process of annexation of Texas and the relations with Mexico.[68]

At the time of his election as president, two forms of Manifest Destiny were present. One of them was a strategy Northeastern in spirit, which was advocated by John O'Sullivan himself. This version aimed for a subtle, gradual process of expansion, which allowed for careful consideration of matters. People behind this idea still believed that, ultimately, expansion would happen. The Northwestern option was more immediate and aggressive, calling for a quick realization of America's divine mission. As we will see, Polk would choose the latter, being the pragmatic, realist politician that he was.[69]

First, let's turn our attention to how the president handled the Oregon issue. In his campaign, he had asserted the "all-Oregon" point and had the full support of his cabinet.[70] Despite the fact that Oregon was a shared territory between the US and Britain, it was predominantly inhabited by Americans and dominated by US merchants, who had been using the region as a gateway to conduct trade in the Pacific. An increased number of migrants came from the heartland of the United States, doubling Oregon's permanent population in 1845. These largely unexplored lands promised a better life to those who sought it. Technological developments, most notably new railroads, greatly reduced the travel time between Oregon and other American states, making the territory less isolated than it had

---

[68] LaFeber (1994), pp. 107-108.

[69] Merk (1995), p. 61.

[70] Merk (1995), p. 63.

been a couple of decades earlier when John Quincy Adams had initially negotiated over it with the British.[71]

In mid-1845, Richard Pakenham, the British minister to Washington, was offered a deal that divided the Oregon Territory along the forty-ninth parallel. The proposal was denied by the minister without even consulting London. This infuriated Polk and caused the British government to disavow the actions of his minister. Britain urged Pakenham to start renegotiations with Polk immediately, but Polk would have none of it. Instead of the forty-ninth parallel, he now demanded all the territory up to 54°40', which was the northernmost US claim. The Democrats were in full support of the new offer. The cries of "Fifty-four forty or fight" were heard in Congress.[72] It was at this time that O'Sullivan coined the term "Manifest Destiny," giving the expansionists further motivation behind their actions.

The British, of course, denied the offer, as giving this much territory to the US would mean giving up a lot of valuable harbors. Instead, in true British fashion, they mobilized their warships in the region, reminding the Americans of their military supremacy and refusing to retreat beyond the forty-ninth. Despite the fact that Polk had great support from the Democrats and that he had reminded Congress of the main principle of the Monroe Doctrine (the region's non-colonization by any European power), he simply did not have an army to match the British in the potential war that he faced, especially considering that, at that point, tensions with Mexico were at their peak. Thus, he gave the matter over to the Senate, which was dominated by the Whigs, who were opposed to aggressive policies. The strategy worked. The United States, led by distinguished senators like John C. Calhoun and Daniel Webster, accepted the forty-ninth parallel compromise. With this, Polk was able to achieve the terms of

---

[71] LaFeber (1994), p. 112.

[72] Merk (1995), pp. 64-65.

the original deal and avoid what would have inevitably become a devastating conflict with Britain.[73]

The handling of the Oregon dispute was seen as a victory for Polk. He had managed to turn a potential catastrophe into a win for Manifest Destiny. However, the events in the South would prove to be more challenging to deal with. Parallel to the negotiations with the British, Polk had to deal with the annexation of Texas—an issue that the previous cabinet of John Tyler had resolved days before Polk's inauguration. It was a more difficult and more consequential matter, and it would directly cause the Mexican-American War.

The Annexation of Texas

After the independence in 1821, US-Mexican relations were pretty friendly. Many Americans aided Mexico voluntarily in its efforts of gaining independence from the Spanish, something they had experienced themselves firsthand in the 1770s when they defeated the British. American sentiment was based on the values of liberty back then, and helping out a struggling new nation that was fighting for its freedom was close to the hearts of the American people. Plus, with the Monroe Doctrine, the US basically indirectly guaranteed the safety of Mexico too. It had asserted that no European colonizers were welcome to take the continent for themselves, which meant that it would oppose not only any Europeans that threatened the United States but also other new nations in the region (even though the United States refused to formally enter an alliance with other newly established Latin American countries).

But the assertion of the Monroe Doctrine was not enough to keep Mexican-American relations strong. Throughout the years, Mexico was busy with its own internal struggles and did not really have much time for implementing a valid foreign policy, especially something that would fit the American preference. The US, on the other hand, had become expansionist, and it strived to spread its divine mission of

---

[73] LaFeber (1994), p. 114.

"liberating" any nations and "teaching" them the fundamentals of what the American people stood for. For many, Manifest Destiny was not only a justification for claiming Oregon, but it also meant someday annexing other territories that were in the interest of the US, including the distant rich lands of California and the much closer Texan lands. John Quincy Adams and Andrew Jackson had even made offers to Mexico for acquiring Texas, but the Mexican government rejected all their proposals.

After 1836, US-American relations would really start to deteriorate. The Texas Revolution in 1836 was essentially a revolution of the emigrant Americans against the Mexican government. As we already discussed, Texas was mostly inhabited by the American people, most of whom included slave-owner Southerners who had followed the lead of Stephen Austin and established many of the Texan settlements. By the time of the revolution, they even outnumbered the Mexican population, and because of the conservative policies of the Mexican government at the time, they decided to rebel for their rights. This is not to say that the Mexican population was not involved in the revolution too. The leading Mexicans in Texas, for instance, were all for the revolution, most notably Juan Seguín, who even commanded a company at the Battle of San Jacinto.[74] The revolutionary movement was prevalent throughout all of Mexico, but in those states nearest to the national capital, the presence of an organized military force under the direction of Santa Anna rendered actual resistance useless.[75] The remoteness and the vastness of the territory was a great advantage for the revolutionary Texans, helping them overcome a much more disciplined and experienced Mexican Army. Despite this, it was widely believed by many Mexicans (and some Americans) that the revolution had been the climax of a carefully orchestrated plan of the

---

[74] Fulmore, Z. T. (1901). "The Annexation of Texas and the Mexican War." The Quarterly of the Texas State Historical Association, 5(1), 28–48.
http://www.jstor.org/stable/27784897. P.35.

[75] Fulmore (1901), p.35.

United States government in an effort to weaken Mexico and take away a big chunk of its territory by later annexing an independent Texas.[76]

Thus, after the revolution, especially after the United States officially recognized Texas in 1837, Mexican-American relations slowly deteriorated. Mexico refused to recognize Texas's independence. General Bustamante, for example, had stated in his address to the Mexican Congress in January of 1838 that "With respect to the Texas campaign, I will only observe that its prosecution is the first duty of the Government and of all Mexicans...What Mexican does not feel in his breast an insuppressible joy on seeing the arms of his nation triumphant ever against a horde of infamous bandits?"[77]

Mexican officials saw the Texans as unlawful rebels who had betrayed their country and their people. However, some thought it would be both unwise and impossible for a struggling Mexico to retake the territory. Most notably, Juan de Dios Cañedo, the foreign minister, had noted that Mexico was incapable of reconquering Texas because of the strong unbreakable spirit of the Texan people, calling them "brave, hardy, and skillful." He firmly believed that Mexico had neither the time nor the means of taking back its lost province, noting the weak, unorganized military of the country, which would have been at a disadvantage against Texas. The only way he thought Mexico would be able to succeed would be by a naval assault, but again, it did not possess the strength or experience of carrying out a marine operation. Cañedo also stated that war with Texas would mean war with the Americans because the US government would not be able to hold off those who would volunteer to defend the territory, as they had done in 1836. In addition, Cañedo recognized that the province of Texas was ultimately unimportant for Mexico:

---

[76] Fulmore (1901), p.29.

[77] Smith, J. H. (1910). "The Mexican Recognition of Texas." The American Historical Review, 16(1), 36–55. https://doi.org/10.2307/1834307

"And for what purpose would all our efforts be made? To subjugate a horde of aliens and recover a province less valuable to us than the least productive of those we still have, only to find it necessary in the end either to exterminate the inhabitants or to settle the matter by negotiation. Many say it is better to continue the war, because if peace be made the Texans will encroach upon us. But in that case all the advantages would lie upon our side. It would be for them to make the long marches, to operate in a foreign country, to contend against an alien race...By making peace with Texas we should secure great benefits at home, and by ending a war that hinders commerce and progress we should gain credit among the nations."[78]

These claims were pretty logical. Mexico simply did not have the time or the ability to reconquer Texas, as was demonstrated in the attempt of 1842. However, few, Cañedo included, dared to oppose the Mexican government. That is why the sentiment of taking back Texas stood largely uncontested.

Despite this, Mexico still refused to recognize Texas's independence. It was natural that it didn't. After all, which country would be proud in publicly acknowledging that they have lost control over a vast portion of their territory? It is possible that if the Mexican government had recognized the independence of Texas, other revolutionary-minded movements would have sprouted in places like California and Yucatán (both of which already had similar independence sentiments and did eventually rebel), creating further chaos in an already chaotic country. It would be a shameful display for Mexico on the international scene too. This is one of the reasons why Mexico was still reluctant to acknowledge the independence of Texas, even after countries like Britain, which held great influence in Mexico at the time, did so (the other reason being that Britain might have wanted the territory for itself and swept in, claiming Texas lawfully or announcing a protectorate without starting a war with Mexico). Thus, when Mexico warned the United States that annexing Texas would

---

[78] Smith (1910), pp. 37-38.

mean war, it believed to be acting justly since it still considered Texas to be a Mexican territory.[79]

The issue of Texas was greatly discussed in the United States too. The annexation sentiment grew in the country as the population and wealth in Texas grew year by year. The first annexation treaty was proposed in 1843. It was opposed by some notable Democrats like John Quincy Adams, who thought acquiring wealthy developing Texas would mean that it would become a slave state, which would greatly disrupt the balance of power that existed between the North and the South. The Whigs were also largely against annexation because of the aggressive Mexican response that claimed that annexation would mean war between the two countries. So, when the treaty was submitted to the Senate in June 1844, it was unable to gain the two-thirds majority it needed to pass.

The American people, however, already regarded Texas as one of the states and the Texans as one of their own. Texans were, in fact, mostly Americans. They had a constitution that was influenced by the US Constitution. They had the same form of government as the United States. They believed in the same ideals as most Americans. This was the main reason behind Polk advocating for the direct annexation of Texas in his presidential campaign. He knew that Texas becoming a US territory was only a matter of time. Polk realized that the American people thought of Texans as being their own and that a big portion of the population desired it to officially become a state.

In response to the public upheaval, in late 1844, President John Tyler drew up a second treaty, a joint resolution aimed at annexing Texas, which, unlike the first treaty, required only a majority of the House and the Senate to be passed. The treaty saw powerful opposition in the Senate while being passed in the House. The main argument against the annexation was that it would certainly lead to war with Mexico. These concerns in the Senate were apparently handled

---

[79] Smith (1910), pp. 38-39.

by Polk, who promised the Whigs who were against the annexation that he would handle the tense relations with Mexico by peacefully discussing and resolving the ongoing border disputes. Eventually, the Senate passed the measure twenty-seven to twenty-five. The United States had voted for annexation. John Tyler set a precedent by acquiring the land through a simple majority.[80] On March 1st, 1845, President Tyler signed the bill, just days before Polk started his term. The treaty was ratified on July 4th, 1845, and agreed to by Texas in October. On December 29th, 1845, Texas would officially become part of the Union.

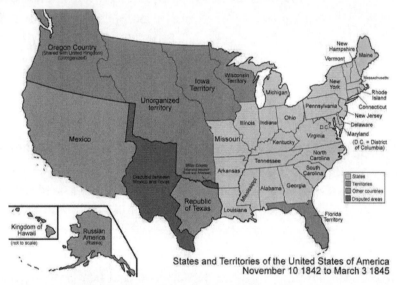

States and Territories of the United States of America
November 10 1842 to March 3 1845

What the United States looked like before Texas was annexed.
(Source: Golbez; Wikimedia Commons)

The annexation greatly altered the political landscape of the continent. For the United States, especially President Polk, it was a victory. Since 1836, the annexation had been an ongoing matter with no real progress until 1843, when the sentiment was revived by Tyler's administration. The Americans saw Texas as a young, free, independent state, one that had been liberated from the tyranny of Mexico. The fact that the revolution in Texas was mainly caused by

---

[80] LaFeber (1994), p. 108.

emigrant Americans contributed to the public sentiment that Texas belonged with the rest of the USA. However, the US government had always been undecided on the matter. President Martin Van Buren had declined Texas's offer to annex the territory since he did not want to further complicate US-Mexican relations and firmly believed that the Constitution did not allow the US to take control over a sovereign, independent nation.[81] Even when Tyler tried to annex Texas in 1844, he failed, causing him to stretch his constitutional powers in early 1845 when he declared the treaty to be a joint resolution. It was of no doubt that the individuals in charge of running the country—the US senators and congressmen—were reluctant to carry out the annexation. They had carefully analyzed the tense political climate at the time and had rightly identified that the annexation of Texas could not solely be based on what the large majority of US citizens desired.

Polk, on the other hand, used the matter during his campaign to defeat his competitors by a razor-thin margin. However, when he entered the office in early March 1845, the annexation bill had already been signed just days before by John Tyler. Still, Polk had to carry out his word of trying to peacefully solve the disputes with Mexico that followed. As we will see later on, he did not keep his promise. In his message on December 2nd, 1845, he stated,

"Texas has declared her independence and maintained it by her arms for more than nine years. She has had an organized government in successful operation during that period. Her separate existence as an independent state has been recognized by the United States and the principal powers of Europe...it had become manifest to the whole world that any further attempt on the part of Mexico to conquer her, or overthrow her government, would be vain...The agreement to acknowledge the independence of Texas, with or without this condition, is conclusive against Mexico. The independence of Texas is a fact, conceded by Mexico herself, and she has no right or

---

[81] Barker, E. C. (1946). "The Annexation of Texas." The Southwestern Historical Quarterly, 50(1), 49–74. http://www.jstor.org/stable/30237259. P. 55.

authority to prescribe restrictions on the form of government which Texas might afterwards choose to assume."[82]

Polk, once again, had shown his aggressive and ambitious side. This statement demonstrated the position that characterized his presidency—the American government would not back down from its divine mission to spread the ideas of liberty and democracy to all. It was the destiny of the American people, and it was used as a justification for the developments that followed.

Mexico, on the other hand, was devastated by the annexation. It meant that the country's desperate efforts to not recognize Texas's independence had been in vain. For years, the chance of taking back Texas had been a motivating factor and a justification for the actions of the Mexican government. For some, like Santa Anna, it was a personal issue that directly came into conflict with his *caudillo* pride. Mexico never took into consideration the advice of other nations to recognize Texas, despite its incapability of reconquering the territory. So, when Texas was stripped away, Mexico faced yet another series of revolts and mass discontent. The government tried everything in its power to persuade the Mexicans (and, to a large degree, itself) that Texas was still a Mexican state. It even threatened war with the United States if the annexation went through, and if Mexico did declare war at the time of the annexation, it probably would have been defeated by the United States.

However, it would ultimately be the border dispute between the state of Texas and Mexico that would cause the Mexican-American War. On one side stood a cunning, aggressively-minded President Polk, who was backed up by the expansionist United States. On the other side was a disoriented, troubled Mexico, which was in the way of the powerful locomotive that was Manifest Destiny.

---

[82] Fulmore (1901), p. 39.

Chapter 5 – The Beginning of the War and Its Opposition in the US

Negotiations for California

President James K. Polk had successfully completed the first promise he had made during his presidential campaign. On December 29th, 1845, Texas officially became the twenty-eighth state of the Union. In parallel, he also saw progress with the matter of Oregon and, as we already mentioned, was able to establish it as a US territory in 1846. However, the expansionist mindset of the president did not stop there. As we will see, Polk was determined to acquire California, a rich, vast, almost fairy-tale-like "promised land." This, paired with the ongoing heated border dispute between the United States and Mexico, would see Polk lead his country into war in May of 1846.

Why was Polk so obsessed with California? Well, he believed that, just like the US had to "re-annex Texas" and "re-occupy Oregon," it also had a valid claim on the region. Once again, Manifest Destiny backed him up, giving him a valid reason for wanting to take control of the province. Divine justification and Polk's personal ambition aside, Americans had indeed established some settlements in the region. California was still a part of Mexico, despite the fact that it was sparsely populated and largely independent, just as Texas had been. By 1845, an estimated one thousand Americans had crossed the country to the distant lands of California. They joined the already existing Americans who lived in the region, who were mainly engaging in the Pacific trade with Russia and the rest of Asia from the towns of San Francisco and San Diego. Unlike the situation in Texas, these settlers were still vastly outnumbered by about seven thousand Spanish-speaking Mexicans, but they still lived in peace. This is why the issue of California was not as popular among the US public. Plus, continuous clashes with the Native American populations that lived in the area in large numbers also made the cries for annexation unpopular. But Polk wanted the land. He wanted to gain control over the rich ports of the region, which would boost trade in the Pacific and please the American merchants who provided for a great portion of the United States' wealth.[83]

A more immediate issue that presented itself with the annexation of Texas was the border dispute between the US and Mexico. The Mexican foreign minister had left Washington on March 7th, 1845, four days after the approval of the annexation by President Tyler, breaking off relations with the US. On July 20th, in the midst of the Texas annexation process, the Mexican government stated that if the annexation went through, it would equate to a declaration of war. However, once again, internal revolts struck the country. Despite the fact that President José Joaquín de Herrera of Mexico was given the authority by the government to go to war, he believed that peaceful negotiations were better. After a brief revolt in the summer of 1845, he managed to take back his seat in September, and Polk sent John Slidell to not only negotiate the border dispute but also offer to buy California and what is now New Mexico. Allegedly, Polk offered Mexico an amount up to $30 million (equal to about $900 million

---

83 LaFeber (1994), p. 115.

today), which was a generous offer considering the fact that the territories Polk wanted to buy were virtually uncontrolled by the Mexicans due to their remoteness. More importantly, he wanted Mexico to recognize the Rio Grande River as the official new border.

Unfortunately for Slidell, President Herrera was in a difficult situation. While he personally opposed war with the US, most of the country, including the absolute majority of the government, raged on about it. The Mexicans were desperate to find some silver lining in the midst of the constant internal fighting, instability, and socioeconomic problems. Many saw reconquering Texas as the only way of getting back some of their pride. So, when Slidell arrived in Mexico City in December, Herrera refused to take him. The Mexican government claimed that Slidell was just a normal envoy from the US, one who was authorized to negotiate all matters instead of being a diplomat focused on the ongoing, more relevant, and pressing matter of the border dispute in Texas.[84] In reality, if the negotiations went through and if the US emerged with its desired outcome of acquiring California and New Mexico, as well as establishing the border along the Rio Grande, it would be another diplomatic catastrophe in the eyes of the Mexican people that would definitely lead to another revolt. Plus, Herrera was already in a weak position and did not wish to jeopardize his seat by being accused of being pro-American.

US-Mexican Border Dispute

It is important to go into details about what both sides thought the official border between them should have been. It is difficult to precisely say which position is correct because the history of the border goes back to the Adams-Onis Treaty of 1819, which decided that the eastern border between the United States and Spain (Mexico was still not independent back then) was to be established at the Sabine River, which still separates the modern-day US states of Texas and Louisiana. When Mexico gained its independence, it, therefore,

---

[84] Fulmore (1901), p. 40.

inherited this border. Under the 1824 constitution, the Mexican state of Coahuila y Tejas stretched from that point in the east to no clearly defined boundary in the west.

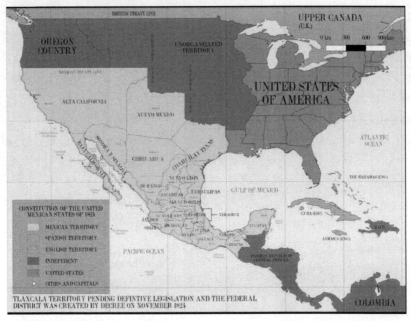

What Mexico looked like in 1824. (Source: Wikimedia Commons)

In 1835, Coahuila and Texas split, and after the Texas Revolution in 1836, the Rio Grande River was unofficially regarded as the border between Mexico and Texas. There are several reasons behind this, the main one being that when Santa Anna was defeated and captured at the Battle of San Jacinto, he retreated his forces west of the Rio Grande in accordance with the first public treaty he made with the newly independent Texans. Mexico, however, would never officially recognize the border because that would mean that it also recognized the independence of Texas. Despite this, Texas did not really control any territory past the Nueces, a smaller river northeast of the Rio Grande.

The whole area between the Nueces and the Rio Grande was disputed. Neither side really had any valuable claims or settlements in the disputed area. San Antonio was the most important Texan town nearest to the Nueces, and it was a couple of hundred miles north. On the easternmost point of the Nueces River, where it joined the Gulf of Mexico, a small town named Corpus Christi was Texas's farthest real outpost. The space in between the two rivers, often called the Trans-Nueces, was not officially governed by either side. After the Texas Revolution, it was briefly claimed by a new rebellious Mexican territory under the name of the Republic of the Rio Grande, which did not last for long. Other than that, neither Texas nor Mexico had made any significant attempts at establishing firm control over the region. Mexico simply did not have enough time to properly invade Texas, and their efforts in 1842 were just small-scale raids that were eventually repelled by the Texans. Texas, on the other hand, had also tried to gain control over a valuable part in the northern part of the territory with the Santa Fe expedition of 1841. However, this effort was also unsuccessful.[85]

All in all, the border dispute was a very sensitive matter. According to over-exaggerated Texan claims, all lands in between the Rio Grande and the Nueces, all the way up to the Rio Grande's source in Colorado, including parts of New Mexico like Santa Fe, belonged to Texas.[86] For Mexico, acknowledgment of such or, as a matter of fact, any existing border with Texas also meant its formal recognition. This, paired with Mexico's decision to cut diplomatic ties with the US and Polk's full support of Texan claims after the annexation, meant that the stage was set for war. The spark was there; it only needed a slight breeze to be set ablaze.

Outbreak of Hostilities

Polk fully understood that war was inevitable. It can even be said that it was a part of his long-term plan, which originated all the way back to his presidential campaign. Remember that he was a simple,

---

[85] Osborn, C. (2015). "The Changing Mexico-US Border." The Library of Congress. https://blogs.loc.gov/maps/2015/12/the-changing-mexico-u-s-border/.

[86] Miller (1996), p. 220.

pragmatic, and astute politician. Remember that he had also convinced the opposing senators to vote for the annexation of Texas by assuring them that he would peacefully try to solve the existing border dispute that would occur. When he became president, he "fulfilled" this promise by sending John Slidell to negotiate with Mexico. However, Slidell's main mission was not to "agree" on any particular border between the now American Texas and Mexico. Slidell was sent to Mexico to propose a purchase of a huge chunk of land that included territory far beyond any valid American claims.

Yes, the province of California and what is now the American Southwest were Mexican regions. While these regions mostly operated on their own, the Mexicans knew that giving them up would only add insult to injury. At the time of Slidell's arrival, the Mexican people were largely motivated to take back control of Texas. They had realized that it had broken off from the rest of the country and that it had taken a portion of Mexican pride in the process. So, when Slidell arrived to negotiate, he was, as expected, unsuccessful. What followed next was a response from Polk that is very logical, considering his proud, ambitious personality—he would fulfill his goal and acquire the desired territory no matter what stood in his way, be it Mexico, his government, or any other circumstance. As historian Walter LaFeber remarks, "The president's policy was both simple and devious. He slowly squeezed Mexico militarily until it struck back."[87]

In parallel to sending Slidell, Polk had ordered General Zachary Taylor to station his troops at the town of Corpus Christi on the Nueces River. Taylor's troops arrived in August, taking a defensive, passive position, and awaited further orders.[88] Mexico had also sent forces to the Rio Grande. After learning that Slidell was in Mexico City to negotiate with President Herrera, General Mariano Paredes, who was in charge of the Mexican forces, returned to the capital and

---

[87] LaFeber (1994), p. 117.

[88] Fulmore (1901), p. 40.

deposed Herrera in December, just one week after Slidell's arrival. Unlike Herrera, Paredes publicly stated that he was in favor of reclaiming what had been lost and strengthened the pro-war sentiment. When Polk received the news of the failed negotiations, as well as Mexico's preparations for war, he reinforced Taylor's force, realizing that the outbreak of hostilities was only a matter of time. Then, in January, he ordered Taylor to move his troops farther up to the Rio Grande, knowing that Mexico had stationed its forces there and was awaiting a potential offensive.[89] Polk had told Taylor to strictly act on the defensive, though. The Mexicans confronted Taylor's troops in March of 1846, who had started building a defensive military fort near the city of Matamoros. The commander of the Mexican forces at Matamoros sent a message to Taylor to immediately retreat with all his forces north of the Nueces River and that any other action by the Americans would be considered hostile. Taylor refused.[90]

Hostilities erupted in April when a Mexican cavalry unit of two thousand ambushed a seventy-men US patrol/scouting force near Matamoros, killing eleven Americans and capturing more than fifty. General Taylor quickly sent word about this to Polk. The Mexicans then proceeded to lay siege to the American fort outside Matamoros in early May, prompting Taylor to answer by mobilizing a force of about 2,400 men. A larger Mexican force intercepted Taylor's movement at the Battle of Palo Alto. However, despite outnumbering the Americans by about a thousand, Taylor managed to defeat the Mexicans due to superior artillery, shattering the Mexican troops and making them retreat. The following day, on May 9th, 1846, the Americans would gain another victory at the Battle of Resaca de la Palma, where the US cavalry managed to outmaneuver the Mexican infantry and capture their artillery. The Mexicans were completely routed and fled south of the Rio Grande, with many dying while crossing the river. All in all, the United States suffered up to two

---

[89] LaFeber (1994), p. 117.

[90] Miller (1996), p. 220.

hundred casualties, and there were at least six hundred killed on the Mexican side. After these confrontations in the spring of 1846, the US emerged victorious.[91]

Zachary Taylor at the Battle of Resaca de la Palma. (Source: Library of Congress; Wikimedia Commons)

When General Taylor's message on the outbreak of the hostilities reached Polk on May 9th, the president immediately urged Congress to declare war. In his address, Polk notoriously stated that "the cup of forbearance had been exhausted"[92] and that "Mexico has passed the boundary of the United States and shed American blood upon the American soil."[93] Polk pointed out that the two countries were already in a state of war with each other. He further claimed that Mexico was the aggressor and that Taylor was trying to defend the newly acquired state of Texas from a Mexican invasion. For these reasons, Polk believed that Congress should officially declare war, which it did on May 13th, 1846.

[91] Heidler, D. S., Heidler, J. T., & Greenwood Press. (2006). *The Mexican War* (Ser. Greenwood Guides to Historic Events, 1500-1900). Greenwood Press. Pp. 63-64.

[92] LaFeber (1994), p. 117.

[93] Miller (1996), p. 221.

Opposition to the War in the US

The House of Representatives overwhelmingly approved of the war bill. The final vote counted 174 ayes and 14 nays, with 35 abstentions. However, it is important to understand that not everyone was as in favor of the war, including many government officials and public figures to different popular journals and editorials. In the House, Polk's decision to declare war was met with harsh criticism not only from the Whigs, whose critical response was natural since they were generally more reserved when it came to aggressive foreign policies, but also from some Democrats, who, despite being in favor of expansion, did not buy the sketchy war proposition that Polk had presented. This was true for virtually all opposing parties. Mainly, many believed that Polk lacked evidence when he claimed that American troops had been slain on American soil. The opposition asserted that the Rio Grande had never really been declared as the official American border. The Trans-Nueces was also not a Mexican territory, making it a disputed region. Therefore, when Polk ordered Taylor to move into the disputed lands, he was the aggressor.[94]

This was one of the main arguments against Polk. According to him, the United States was in a defensive war since it was Mexico who had struck first when they ambushed Taylor's seventy-men patrol force. But the opposition saw Polk as the provocateur. The *National Intelligencer*, for example, a leading Whig organ, asserted that he had handled the disputed border issue unnecessarily aggressively and violated the constitutional powers granted to the president.[95] Later on, this position was further supported by future President Ulysses S. Grant, who served as a lieutenant in Taylor's army during the war. Being a firsthand witness of the events that led to the outbreak of the war, Grant wrote in his memoirs, "We were sent to provoke a fight,

---

[94] Merk (1995), p. 89.

[95] Lawrence, N. (2013). "'This boa-constrictor appetite of swallowing states and provinces': Anti-Imperialist Opposition to the U.S./Mexican War." South Central Review, 30(1), 55–82. http://www.jstor.org/stable/44016818. P. 5.

but it was essential that Mexico should commence it...Mexico showing no willingness to come to the Nueces to drive the invaders from her soil, it became necessary for the 'invaders' to approach to within a convenient distance to be struck...It was desirable to occupy a position near the largest centre of population possible to reach, without absolutely invading territory to which we set up no claim whatever."[96]

In addition, a significant portion of the opposition was largely motivated by racist and nativist sentiments. According to these views, the Mexicans were seen as undeveloped, inferior Catholics who were unfit to be integrated into the advanced United States, which was dominated by Anglo-American Protestants. John C. Calhoun, for example, a notable Democrat and a South Carolina senator, did not believe the Mexicans were ready to become "American" (it is needless to say that everyone in the US firmly believed that they would emerge victorious in the war; hence their assertions already take this into consideration). On the Senate floor, while addressing his peers, Calhoun asked the question, "Are the Mexicans fit to be politically associated with us? Are they fit not only to govern themselves, but for governing us also? Are any of you, Senators, willing that your State should constitute a member of the Union of which twenty-odd Mexican States, more than one-third of the whole, would be a part?"[97]

This view directly clashed with Manifest Destiny. It presented the United States as an aggressive conqueror and an enforcer of democratic ideals, not as a peaceful liberator. Despite the US insisting that it was destined by God to spread liberty and democracy among the peoples of the continent, it had never really been at war with a foreign nation where it had to use force to convince foreigners to embrace American principles. Yes, Manifest Destiny had caused the colonization of distant lands and, more often than not, the forceful displacement of Native Americans from their original habitats, but

[96] Widger, D. (2018). "Memoirs of General U. S. Grant."
https://www.gutenberg.org/files/4367/4367-h/4367-h.htm

[97] Lawrence (2013), p. 57.

that was virtually it. Gaining Oregon had taken a peaceful albeit tense agreement with Britain. But Mexico was a sovereign republic with a population that was considered inferior to the American people. So, when it came to going to war with an actual independent country to (potentially) conquer much of its territory and integrate its people into American society, many Americans thought that the effort was not worth it since it would take years for the conquered Mexicans to adjust to the American way of life.

The slavery issue was also something that caused disagreement between the different parties. Many realized that when the United States would win the war (remember that this was basically a given), problems would arise when deciding where slavery would be legal and where it would not. Polk had failed to understand this factor himself and tried to maintain his position that the war (US foreign policy) and slavery (a domestic issue) were two separate things that could not be associated with each other. In reality, however, the two matters were closely intertwined. What would happen when the US got a hold of the vast portion of the land it had desired? How would the practice of slavery be determined in these territories? The Mexican people were anti-slavery themselves, so making any acquired Mexican-dominated territories slavery states (which was the case in virtually all the desired lands) would be problematic. Plus, technically, according to the Missouri Compromise of 1820, the acquired Mexican lands would all fall south of the designated line, complicating the matters even more and leaving politicians wondering if the Missouri Compromise was still adequate (after all, when it had been designed, the US was not nearly as big as it was during the war with Mexico).[98]

---

[98] LaFeber (1994), p. 120.

Chapter 6 – The Mexican-American War

Taylor's Offensive

When Polk declared war on May 13th, 1846, he simultaneously ordered different US commanders to attack on different fronts. Taylor and his troops had already seen progress over the Rio Grande, defeating the Mexicans in the first encounters of the war without any significant casualties. Taylor already had a foothold in the Mexican territory, which was to be swiftly utilized by Polk. In two months' time, Polk would reinforce Taylor's army with troops from San Antonio, and Taylor would start moving toward the valuable Mexican town of Monterrey, close to the Rio Grande, in the northeastern part of Mexico. Gaining control over the town would be a great deal for the Americans since it would provide them with valuable supplies and a potential fallback position if they failed to advance farther.

Six thousand American troops reached Monterrey in September. After learning that about seven thousand Mexican soldiers were present in the town, fortifying their position and getting ready to defend it from the Americans, Taylor proceeded to attack quickly. Despite the fact that they were outnumbered, the Americans still possessed superior horse artillery, which was an advantage in sieges.

Besides, most of Mexican General Pedro de Ampudia's forces were cavalrymen who were inexperienced in fighting on foot, which would be necessary when the Americans reached the city's streets. Thus, when Taylor ordered his troops to attack on September 20th, he managed to win the siege in just four days. Surprisingly, however, Taylor received an armistice proposal from Ampudia, according to which the Mexicans would give up the city with the small remainder of their forces retreating south for about forty miles. Taylor agreed to this proposal, and the truce between the two forces would last for eight weeks.

American troops marching on Monterrey. (Source: Wikimedia Commons)

Despite the fact that Monterrey was a clear victory for the US, Taylor had hoped that the negotiations with Ampudia and the fact that he had seized the city would lead to actual peace negotiations with Mexico. He was wrong. His orders never were to conquer Mexico, but it was what President Polk ultimately desired. Taylor believed that with his three quick victories, the border dispute would be settled because he had driven the Mexican forces out of the area. However, he failed to understand that Polk had only used the border dispute as a (somewhat valid) *casus belli* for his war with Mexico. His real goal was not only to drive the Mexicans south of the Rio Grande but also to capture California and New Mexico for the US. Therefore, Taylor's hopes that his success would lead to peace were way off. There was another factor on the Mexican side that Taylor did not take into consideration. It was the return of none other than Santa Anna.[99]

The Return of Santa Anna

Our favorite *caudillo* had been in exile in Cuba for quite some time after a failed military coup back home. As always, Santa Anna was never completely out of the loop. So, when Polk secretly sent him an agent in July of 1846, he listened to what the Americans had to say. Santa Anna negotiated with Polk, convincing him that if he managed to return home, he would try to seize the government once again and advocate for peace. Polk, in return, wanted the disputed border territory and New Mexico. Santa Anna vehemently agreed to anything he was proposed and even tried to give the Americans some valuable information about how to attack different Mexican cities like Tampico. Eventually, because of his friendly and passionate attitude, he landed in Veracruz in August, being let through by American ships that had been blockading the eastern Mexican coast.[100]

At the time of his arrival, the Mexican government was in tatters. General Paredes, who had become president during Slidell's visit to Mexico City, could not gain popular support because of his defeats at Palo Alto and Resaca de la Palma. In addition, he had failed to urge the Mexican Congress to officially declare war, despite acquiring the command of all forces. His term was doomed, and Santa Anna was there to take advantage of it. Crucially, when Paredes left the capital to personally lead the army against the Americans, his government in Mexico City was overthrown.

Thus, the stage was once again set for Santa Anna. Through his agents, he managed to get an unofficial alliance with the former

---

[99] Heidler (2006), p. 87.

[100] Miller (1996), p. 225.

president and the leader of the liberals, Gómez Farías. Farías and his supporters had overthrown the previous government. They installed José Mariano Salas as interim president, who, together with Farías, worked on gaining public support for Santa Anna's return, as well as reinstituting the people's trust in the government, which had stripped away many civil liberties during Paredes's strict rule, such as the freedom of the press. According to the plan, Santa Anna would take charge of the army, as he was the most experienced and decorated general Mexico had. Despite the fact that upon his arrival, he was received with mixed feelings, Santa Anna managed to gain the much-needed support of the people. The (in)famous savior of the Mexican people had returned once again in their darkest hour, being seen as the last hope for the country.[101]

Unsurprisingly, however, Santa Anna did not keep his promise to the US. Yes, he did manage to regain power, but he most definitely was not going to use it to start the peace negotiations with the Americans. Such an act would be seen as foolish in the eyes of the Mexican people, whose sentiments for reclaiming the lost territories had been invigorated by the recent defeats. Santa Anna's plan was to sway the general public opinion to his side and reorganize a splintered war effort, after which he would proceed to drive the Americans out of the country, reclaiming his hero status in the process. It is fascinating that he fooled the Americans once again with nearly the exact same proposition from the decade before after his defeat during the Texas Revolution. On the other hand, Polk really had nothing to lose when it came to negotiating with Santa Anna. Everybody already believed that the war effort would be eventually successful, so it would be a great success if they could avoid months of bloodshed and reach their goals peacefully. As we will see later on, Santa Anna would personally lead the Mexican forces against the Americans, drawing out

---

[101] Heidler (2006), pp. 79-80.

the war as much as he could and fighting until there was nothing else to fight for.[102]

Going for Santa Fe

In parallel to Taylor's advance to Monterrey, Polk had ordered Colonel Stephen W. Kearny to start mobilizing his troops. Colonel Kearny was stationed at Fort Leavenworth, which was close to the border with the New Mexico province. Polk had ordered him to protect the trade that went through the area since it might become a target for a potential Mexican offensive. In reality, Kearny would learn later that Polk wanted him to open up another front with the Mexicans in what is today the US Southwest by first taking control of the valuable city of Santa Fe and then moving his attention to California.

Colonel Kearny was an experienced professional. Upon receiving orders to mobilize, he promptly waited for around one thousand volunteers from Missouri to join his ranks, and he began planning for what would eventually be a very long and troublesome march through New Mexico. Kearny and his forces struggled to traverse the vast province on their way to Santa Fe. Due to supply shortages that were caused by the sparsity of settlements in the area, they faced a lot of difficulties, especially when it came to inexperienced volunteers who were not used to traveling in such harsh conditions. Despite this, they managed to adapt to the situation because of the training and advice they would receive from Kearny himself and his regular forces. In addition, they were very eager and motivated to go through any hardships for the sake of Manifest Destiny. Many had joined the army solely because they firmly believed that they were helping accomplish the mission of the United States of spreading the ideals of liberty throughout the continent. Their sheer will and perseverance, despite having virtually no real war experience, largely existed because they

---

[102] Heidler (2006), p. 74.

had a unifying idea—something that the Mexican soldiers did not possess.[103]

Kearny would start his march in early June of 1846. By the first days of August, his army had grown in size, reaching about 2,500 troops. This number included the only religious unit in US history: the Mormon Battalion. Although its role in the war was minor, the men of the battalion still made an impact on the war effort. They aided Kearny's men and constructed Fort Moore. During their time in the war, they learned irrigation techniques from local tribes, which would aid them in their future settlements in Utah. On top of this, the men stumbled upon the Donner Party's campsite (a group of settlers who had moved westward but had to resort to cannibalism to stay alive during the harsh winter months). The men of the Mormon Battalion were the ones who buried the bodies.

On August 18th, Kearny would occupy the city of Santa Fe without firing a single shot; his troops marched into the city and claimed it without any resistance. The reason behind this was the absence of a real, competent leader that would put up any realistic defense against the US. Due to the remoteness of the region from the capital, the Mexican officials had effectively self-governed the area for quite some time. The central government could not really spread its influence there, so when they were confronted with the American guns, the Mexicans peacefully surrendered.

Kearny proceeded to organize an American government in the city, introducing a new law code and an American governor who would govern after he left. For Kearny, it seemed that the path to Santa Fe was much more problematic than actually capturing the city. Ultimately, on September 25th, 1846, Kearny and the majority of his forces set out westward to continue the war effort in California. In a span of two months, he had managed to take control over one of the most valuable cities near the Mexican-American border without any

---

[103] Heidler (2006), pp. 69-70.

fighting, and he was ready to advance farther to help out on another American offensive.[104]

The Conquest of California

After securing Santa Fe and the rest of New Mexico for the US with no serious fighting, Colonel Kearny decided to split his forces. He left Colonel Sterling Price as their commander to ensure the order that he had established in the region would be maintained. Then he set out to join another American military campaign to secure California for the US. The peace was maintained in Santa Fe for quite some time, but eventually, a small Mexican rebellion struck, which was quickly taken care of by the Americans at the beginning of 1847. Thus, New Mexico was firmly under American control. Next on the list were the rich lands of distant California, which seemed closer than ever.

The Californian campaign was unorganized, to say the least. Troubled by the lack of quick communication, the different armies that were involved in taking California for the US had a tough time establishing clear motives and goals. For example, when Kearny left for California in late September 1846, much of the fighting had already happened, and the Americans had already gained a valuable foothold, having occupied big Californian cities. Let's take a look at how the events unfolded.

Commodore John D. Sloat, who was in charge of the US naval forces in the Pacific, had received a message from President Polk prior to the outbreak of the hostilities with Mexico. According to Polk's orders, there was a high probability of war breaking out because of the annexation of Texas. If that were to happen, Sloat's orders were to take San Francisco, an important Californian port. So, when word reached him on May 17th, 1846, that fighting had broken out in Texas, he prepared his ships to take the city.

---

[104] Heidler (2006), pp. 72-73.

At the same time, another American force was present in the region. This was a relatively small topographical expedition led by John C. Frémont, an experienced explorer and the son of a senator. His original mission was to explore the Oregon Territory, which bordered California. The Oregon deal hadn't yet been finalized with the British, but Frémont had been sent there to find new river routes, potential places to settle, and generally study the area. However, for no real reason, Frémont decided to enter the Sacramento Valley in December of 1845 instead of continuing on his march to Oregon.[105] He and his company claimed that they had taken a wrong turn in their journey and headed for Monterey (not to be confused with Monterrey, a Mexican town on the Texan front) to resupply. The expedition was received in Monterey, but Frémont and his forces did not leave for quite some time, despite the Mexican officials providing them with all the supplies they had requested. Although the force was not enough to cause an insurrection that would be problematic, the Mexican authorities still did not enjoy the presence of armed American soldiers in the city.[106]

The suspicions of the Mexicans came true when Frémont led the revolt of the American settlers of northern California, who organized a small force of about three hundred men in early July and declared their independence, proclaiming a new nation named the "Bear Flag Republic." They were named this due to the banner they used, which had an image of a grizzly bear on it. Well, technically, the settlers had a revolt of their own and were joined by Frémont and his men later, but there is reason to believe that during his long stay at Monterey, he had agitated and motivated the American Californians to rebel by secretly meeting with them on a number of occasions. The Mexican response to the rebellion was ineffective. The officials believed that

---

[105] Walker, D. L. (1999). *Bear Flag Rising: The Conquest of California, 1846*. New York: Forge. P. 107.

[106] Heidler (2006), p. 96.

the revolt was backed by the American government, and they were surprised by the drive of the rebelling Americans.[107]

Concurrently, Commodore Sloat was slowly but surely mobilizing his navy for an attack on the Californian ports. His efforts were so slow, in fact, that before he would set sail for San Francisco, which had been his original target, he received official orders to seize Monterey as well. The new orders also clarified to put the captured cities under a "government sponsored by the United States." Thus, Sloat reached Monterey on July 1st. He quickly captured the city around the same time he heard about the Bear Flag Revolt, which had happened in the northern part of California. On July 7th, he declared the whole of California had been annexed for the United States, despite the fact that this was neither true nor his original order from the government. In addition, he sent out word to the rebelling Americans in Sonoma, a city north of San Francisco, to join him in securing the rest of California for the US instead of becoming independent. Many rebels were swayed, including Frémont himself, and they abandoned their independence movement to join the American forces.[108]

About a week later, Sloat was replaced by Commodore Robert F. Stockton, his scheduled successor who arrived and took control of the American forces on July 15th, 1846. Unlike the slow and indecisive Sloat, Stockton was a more aggressive, firm, and strong-willed commander, and he was willing to accelerate the process of conquering all of California. After his arrival, he put Frémont officially in charge of the Bear Flag rebels, who had become volunteers for the US cause. He quickly secured the northern part of California and set his eyes on the south, namely on Los Angeles and San Diego. According to Stockton's plan, he would send Frémont to San Diego, south of Los Angeles, while he and the remainder of the forces would

---

[107] Heidler (2006), p. 98.

[108] Heidler (2006), pp. 98-99.

attack Los Angeles from the north, attacking any Mexican forces that might have tried to defend the city from two sides.[109]

However, the southern parts of California were still under Mexican control. The Mexican officials had observed the developments in Monterey and San Francisco, including the change of command into the hands of Stockton, and they expected an offensive on Los Angeles. Mexican General José María Castro and the governor Pío Pico wanted to defend the remaining Mexican territories. Because of their remoteness from Mexico City, as well as the autonomy that they largely practiced outside of the central Mexican government and the fact that the main Mexican Army was still unorganized, they expected no help. To Pico and other wealthy Californios—the Mexican residents of the province—losing to the Americans may mean the loss of their private property too. They had grown weary of the influx of the Americans over the years, fearing that California could become the new Texas. Some were even convinced that the Americans would force them to convert to Protestantism and bring back slavery to the region if they managed to conquer it. Even with the apparent opposition against the US and its ways, Pico and Castro only managed to muster up to one hundred men. It was a small and unprofessional force, and it would be unable to do anything against Stockton's troops. By the first week of August, when the Americans landed near Los Angeles and an invasion was imminent, hopeless Castro and Pico fled south without putting up a fight. Just like Kearny in Santa Fe, Stockton managed to enter Los Angeles and claim it for the United States on August 13th without firing a single shot.[110]

That is not to say that the Californios did not put up a fight. Soon after the capture of Los Angeles, Stockton decided to declare all of California officially annexed by the United States, something that only Congress had the power to do. After this, he left only about fifty men as the city's garrison, taking the rest of the men with him on a final

---

[109] Walker (1999), p. 154.

[110] Heidler (2006), pp. 100-101.

conquest of the western coast of Mexico. The Californios, seeing that they could easily overpower the small garrison that was left behind, quickly took up arms and drove the forces outside of the city. After hearing what had happened in Los Angeles, Stockton decided to shift his base to San Diego, sending Frémont north to Monterey to deal with yet another potential rebellion. According to the plan, Frémont would return after overviewing the situation at Monterey and take back Los Angeles together with Stockton's forces. The Mexicans knew what was coming, so they tried delaying any American offensive by sending out small cavalry raids to quickly engage American outposts and then retreat. For a while, the hostilities ceased in California.[111]

Finally, after two long months, Colonel Kearny finally arrived in California with a relief force of about three hundred men. In disbelief that Stockton had lost control over Los Angeles and after receiving word that the Mexicans, under the command of Captain. Andrés Pico, were at San Pascual, Kearny set out to meet them in battle. The short Battle of San Pascual took place on December 6th, 1846, when Kearny's troops attacked the Mexican camp in the morning.[112] However, the Mexicans managed to regroup, killing eighteen and wounding about a dozen, Kearny included (his wounds were minor, though). Kearny's men had never fought the Mexican cavalry before and were already exhausted from the long march from Santa Fe. Therefore, the casualties that the Californios managed to inflict caused them to retreat. They eventually reached San Diego on December 12th.

San Pascual was one of the first real Mexican victories in the war. But it did not have the effects the Mexicans would have hoped for. After arriving at San Diego, Kearny and Stockton joined forces and decided to take back Los Angeles. The two commanders did have severe disagreements, with Kearny believing that he should have been

---

[111] Heidler (2006), p. 101.

[112] Heidler (2006), p. 102.

in charge of the army since he was acting on official orders from the government. However, despite their differences, Stockton and Kearny embarked with about six hundred men on an expedition to reclaim Los Angeles after Kearny was fully healed.

Their expedition was also troubled by Mexican raiders, who knew that they did not stand a chance at defending the city against the Americans at full strength. So, they tried to slow them down, but their efforts were ultimately unsuccessful. When the Americans reached the city, the Californios wanted to negotiate but were denied. Equipped with superior artillery and more manpower, Stockton and Kearny broke through the Mexican defense and claimed Los Angeles once again on January 10th, 1847. The retreating Mexican forces were cut off by Frémont and his men, whose journey from Monterey to Los Angeles had been very slow. The United States had managed to occupy every valuable town in California. By the end of January, Stockton's replacement, Commodore W. Branford Shubrick, arrived and took control of the operations. He transferred the command of the army to Colonel Kearny and set up a civil government in California.[113]

Battle of Buena Vista

The defeats on both fronts were devastating for Santa Anna, who was still trying to regain his power and organize the Mexican Army to respond to the American offensive. California was far away from Mexico City, so losing control over it was not as alarming as General Taylor's advance at the Rio Grande, which posed a much more immediate threat. Santa Anna knew that if he wanted to remain in power and further restore his hero status in the eyes of the Mexican people, he needed to act. However, assembling a competent army proved to be a near-impossible task for the *caudillo*. The professional soldiers that he had at his disposal were demoralized from the defeats at the Rio Grande, and the new conscripts that joined the army were

---

[113] Walker (1999), p. 246.

neither experienced nor properly armed to constitute a strong, well-functioning military. In addition to this were the financial problems Mexico was facing. Santa Anna had virtually no available funds to finance his efforts. Even with all of these problems, he hoped that a decisive victory against Taylor would cause a shift in the hearts of both the Mexican and American people. Santa Anna knew that Polk faced a lot of internal opposition to the war, and he believed that the American president would much rather negotiate a deal over the desired territories than continue fighting. Therefore, he appointed himself in charge of the army and shifted the military headquarters to San Luis Potosí, which is north of Mexico City. Knowing that he had little time to act, Santa Anna hoped that a surprise attack would work. He hoped to catch the Americans off-guard and break Taylor's forces, which he heard was far fewer in number. So, in late January of 1847, with an estimated number of about twenty thousand men, he set out to meet Taylor in battle.[114]

On the other side, despite his initial success at the battles at the Rio Grande, General Taylor was also facing some issues. He had broken the eight-week armistice he had agreed to with General Ampudia and moved forward, occupying the town of Saltillo. Even though President Polk was initially satisfied with Taylor, he did not support his offensive anymore. He believed that Taylor had lost too many men at Monterrey and thought that the best way to break Mexico was to gain access to its heartland by landing on its eastern coast and then advancing to Mexico City. That was why he sent General Winfield Scott to organize a naval offensive in the Mexican territories instead of reinforcing General Taylor's army. His displeasure toward Taylor can also be explained by the fact that Taylor was a Whig—a member of the party that vehemently opposed the war's continuation.

For all these reasons, Taylor was ordered to send a portion of his already depleted force to join General Scott, who was assembling his troops at Tampico. Taylor, of course, was not pleased with the

[114] Heidler (2006), pp. 109-110.

situation he found himself in. He wanted to secure more of northern Mexico for the US before a good number of his men left to join Scott's army. In addition, he heard the news of Santa Anna assembling his forces and starting his march northward. So, instead of thinning his numbers even more by splitting up the forces, Taylor organized a defensive position at Buena Vista with about five thousand men.[115]

Santa Anna arrived to meet Taylor in battle on February 22nd, 1847. Santa Anna's forces, despite suffering from desertion, which reduced its numbers by about three thousand men, still massively outnumbered Taylor's army three to one. Santa Anna demanded Taylor to surrender, with the American general refusing. He believed that they had chosen a perfect defensive position; it was a narrow valley surrounded by hills, which could be used advantageously to bombard the Mexican troops with the superior American artillery. Santa Anna, however, expected Taylor's response and already had his battle plans ready. He hoped to split up the American forces by attacking multiple flanks and causing Taylor's defense to stretch itself too thin. Santa Anna's main focus was to break the Americans, believing that his superior numbers would be difficult to repel by the smaller albeit more experienced force.

The fighting began in the afternoon when Santa Anna ordered an assault on the left flank of Taylor's army. This initial attack was repulsed by Taylor. The next morning, however, Santa Anna's men attacked the center of Taylor's troop, overwhelming them with pure numbers. Realizing that the Mexicans were about to break through, Taylor retreated, taking an even more defensive position. He was desperate to defeat the Mexican forces with the help of his artillery. This last-ditch effort worked. For the next several hours, Santa Anna was not able to break through the American defense. The momentum seemed to shift in favor of the Americans, who bought enough time for the artillery to inflict serious casualties on the Mexican ranks. The

[115] Heidler (2006), p. 110.

fighting stopped by the end of the day on February 23rd. Both sides lost many men. Even so, the remaining Mexican troops were still superior in numbers. However, Santa Anna did not order another assault on the American position. He knew that the fighting was over. His troops, who were already fatigued and demoralized, could not withstand another offensive that would be met by American guns.[116]

The Battle of Buena Vista *by Carl Nebel. (Source: Wikimedia Commons)*

No clear victor had emerged immediately after the fighting. Ultimately, Taylor had managed to hold his position, despite suffering heavy casualties. Back home, the battle was at first received as a humiliating defeat, but people soon realized that Taylor had basically achieved the impossible. Even though he had lost a lot of men in the process, Taylor defended the position against a much larger Mexican force, eventually driving them out. Had he lost, who knew what Santa Anna would have done next or where else he would have confronted the Americans in battle. What happened instead was a retreat by Santa Anna. The *caudillo* knew that the result of the battle was less than favorable for him and that if the news of this reached Mexico

---

[116] Heidler (2006), p. 112.

City, the people would be disappointed. That is why he sent word back to the capital, declaring the battle to be a decisive victory and saying that he would pursue the remainder of Taylor's men to crush them fully. However, he instead retreated back to San Luis Potosí to reassemble and prepare to further defend Mexico.[117] While Buena Vista stopped Taylor, it also made him a national hero in the US— something that would help him in his presidential campaign in the years to come. On the other hand, Santa Anna had only delayed the American offensive since the fighting would continue in the east, which was led, this time, by General Winfield Scott.

The Siege of Veracruz

Santa Anna would return to Mexico City when he heard of the news of yet another revolt against the acting president, Gómez Farías. Farías had the difficult task of financing the war effort, and his methods managed to upset all the different radical groups in Mexico. Most notably, it was his decision to seize the property of the church to pay for the war that was regarded as the most reckless. People protested all throughout the city, causing a rebellion that was joined by many military officers and upper-class men. Thus, it was Santa Anna's time to shine once again. He entered the city as a hero after his "victory" against the Americans and took back control, giving the church its properties back and eliminating Gómez Farías as a political actor by making Congress abolish the vice presidency. With the internal bickering somewhat settled, next on the menu was defending the country against a new American offensive in the east.

Veracruz was General Winfield Scott's target, who was now in charge of commanding the main American army. He had been gathering his forces on the eastern Mexican coast at Matamoros and Tampico, while the US Navy, which had been blockading the coast for months, was tasked with scouting the perfect landing site for the operation. The navy, however, did not have enough ships to transport

---

[117] Heidler (2006), p. 113.

all of Scott's troops at once since he had around ten thousand men. Scott did not want to wait a long time to attack. The reason behind this was that summer on the coast was yellow fever season—a deadly disease that would be problematic to take care of, especially because most of Scott's troops had never even encountered it due to its prominence in the coastal regions. Scott believed that he had until May, at the latest, to take Veracruz and advance away from the coast and into the heartland of Mexico to avoid the disease. So, when the navy informed him of the best landing spot at Collado Beach, south of the city, he loaded up his transports and started landing on March 9th, 1847. Establishing their positions on the beach should have been the most difficult part of the operation; however, the landing was met with no resistance from the Mexicans, who did not have any defenses on that part of the beach. Scott managed to land in Mexico with the biggest and most capable American force without losing a single man.[118]

The defense at Veracruz was unreliable. Even though General Juan Morales, the Mexican general in charge of Veracruz, had about 3,300 men at his disposal, he knew that his men were no match for the professional Americans. The artillery he possessed was also vastly inferior. However, he hoped that he could at least delay Scott, believing that the main Mexican force with Santa Anna would eventually manage to regroup and send some help or at least defeat the Americans after Veracruz. Thus, on March 22nd, when General Scott asked him to surrender, he declined. General Scott then proceeded to set up his forces for a siege of the city. For the next two days, Scott would receive additional artillery pieces from the navy, which were much larger and packed a stronger punch than anything Mexico had. He started the heavy bombardment of the city, shelling Veracruz for five straight days. A large portion of the town was completely destroyed, and with the growing civilian unrest, Morales knew there was no way to defend the city. Despite the fact that he was

---

[118] Heidler (2006), pp. 115-118.

afraid of Santa Anna's wrath, he surrendered the city to the Americans on March 29th, 1847.

Scott paroled and allowed the Mexican soldiers and officers to leave the city and set up a temporary military government. He guaranteed the locals' rights and treated them with respect, knowing that it would be best to have peaceful relations with the Mexicans. Scott had successfully carried out the biggest naval landing of the US up to that point, and he captured the valuable city of Veracruz with his army still intact. He also managed to pacify the Mexicans, almost guaranteeing that they would not rebel in the future. Scott's final goal was Mexico City, and the biggest challenge ahead of him was Santa Anna and the Mexican Army.

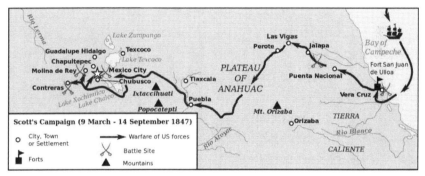

Winfield Scott's campaign in September. (Source: Kaidor; Wikimedia Commons)

The Battle of Cerro Gordo and the March to Mexico City

Capturing Veracruz gave the United States direct access to the Mexican heartland. Scott wanted to start marching toward Mexico City as soon as he could; he was afraid that if he got delayed, yellow fever would take its toll on the army. That is why he wanted to get away from the coast and go deeper into Mexican territory—to avoid the spread of the deadly disease. The other problem he had to eventually face was Santa Anna and the main Mexican force. Despite what had happened at Buena Vista, Santa Anna should not have been underestimated. With all of this in mind, Scott waited in Veracruz long enough to properly resupply for the long march to Mexico City. Then he prepared his vanguard of about three thousand, men led by General David Twiggs, who set out westward via the main road to Mexico City. Twiggs's job was to establish a secure path for the main army, and he was pretty successful, as no Mexican forces attacked the vanguard. However, as Twiggs reached a narrow pass at Cerro Gordo, he noticed the signs of the Mexican Army's presence. Afraid that he would be ambushed, he did not advance any farther through the pass, sending word back to the main force of a potential threat that lay in wait. And Twiggs was completely right.[119]

On the Mexican side, Santa Anna blamed the loss of Veracruz on General Morales, despite not sending him any help. He knew that Mexico had done little to prepare for an American invasion from the east. To his surprise, the American threat, which was now more apparent than ever, made the various groups that were vying for power set aside their differences. They united, more or less, to prepare the capital's defenses together. Due to the new incentives of conscription, the army grew in numbers, and Santa Anna was expected to defeat Scott and put an end to the war. The *caudillo* realized that in an even battle, he would lose against the Americans; they both outgunned and outmatched his force. He also realized that he needed to delay their advance as long as he could, acknowledging the potential of yellow fever developing among Scott's ranks. Thus, on April 2nd, 1847, he took his army east to encamp at Cerro Gordo. This was a good defensive site because the main road that went through it was surrounded by hills, which was where he set up his artillery. There, Santa Anna lay in wait for Scott. If he could not defeat him, at least he could halt his advance long enough for the disease to spread.[120]

After receiving word from Twiggs about a spotted ambush, General Scott did not fancy his chances in battle. The position was impossible to take without major casualties. Instead of advancing and

[119] Heidler (2006), pp. 121-122.

[120] Heidler (2006), p. 121.

engaging directly in battle, he sent his engineers to find an alternate path or a potential weakness he could exploit. The engineers returned with the news that Santa Anna's left flank had the least defenses and that if the US forces could take control of it, they could set up their superior artillery in a way to rain hell upon the Mexican soldiers. Scott did just that. On April 17th, after vicious fighting, the American division led by Twiggs managed to gain control of the flank and, therefore, the rear of the Mexicans. What followed next was a full retreat of the Mexican forces as they were bombarded by the American guns from the hills that they had planned to use themselves. Santa Anna managed to flee, while most of the supplies and possessions of the Mexicans were seized by Scott's men, who stood victorious once again. Santa Anna's plan to delay the Americans had failed. Next was Mexico City.[121]

After Cerro Gordo, Scott continued his march. He reached the second biggest Mexican city of Puebla in early May and took control of the city without any armed resistance. The main problem that presented itself to Scott was the fact that he needed to wait for reinforcements. The volunteers who had joined his army needed to sail back home through Veracruz, as their terms had expired. As they left Scott's ranks, the army was reduced to about seven thousand men, which was not enough to decisively defeat the Mexicans in battle and capture the capital. It was frustrating but necessary to wait for reinforcements.[122]

While at Puebla, General Scott received a potential offer for peace for an initial payment of $10,000 and then $1,000,000 when the war ended. The Mexican messenger claimed that the money would be used to convince the government to vouch for peace instead of continuing the war effort. General Scott did not fully trust the offer because he knew of Santa Anna's capability to deceive the Americans. He consulted his council, which also included Nicholas Trist, the

---

[121] Heidler (2006), p. 122.

[122] Heidler (2006), p. 123.

chief clerk of the State Department who had been specifically sent by Polk to conduct potential peace deals in the name of Washington. Trist was in favor of paying the amount, which was available at the moment in cash as part of the "secret service fund." After considering the offer, the Americans paid the amount and hoped for the best.

Unsurprisingly, the $10,000 payment did not achieve anything. Scott never even heard of the money being given to Santa Anna or to any other Mexican official. In fact, the deal was not even an official offer from the Mexican government. The news of Santa Anna's real defeat at Buena Vista had reached Mexico, and when paired with the obvious defeat at Cerro Gordo, the *caudillo* was struggling to keep his power. He had practically lost the support of Congress—the only institution that was authorized to send an official peace deal. Plus, the public was largely demoralized from fighting, and as the Americans moved closer, the peace sentiment started increasing among the Mexicans. The majority still wanted to fight to restore their pride, but realistically, they knew they did not stand a chance against the United States. In the wake of all this, it is believed that if it really was Santa Anna who had sent the offer for $10,000, he used it to bribe government officials to support the war effort and his presidency. After somewhat consolidating his position, Santa Anna started mobilizing the defenses for Mexico City.[123]

The Fall of Mexico City

By early August of 1847, Scott had finally received more reinforcements at Puebla. Seeing that the $10,000 he had spent for a potential peace treaty was in vain, he started to organize for a final march to the Mexican capital. The new volunteers significantly refreshed his numbers, and on August 7th, after months of being stationed at Puebla, the American force started making its way to Mexico City with one goal in mind—to finally end the war.

---

[123] Heidler (2006), pp. 125-127.

Scott's journey to Mexico City was troubled by guerilla attacks that tried to weaken the American ranks. Approaching the city was a difficult task. Mexico City had a convenient geographical location, with natural barriers that were tricky to overcome with a direct assault. Still, the best way to get to the city was from the south. In addition, Santa Anna had managed to mobilize most of his forces to make it as difficult for Scott to take the city. He knew that he would eventually be defeated, but at least he was willing to give the Americans a hard time.

On August 19th, while Scott's vanguard was still trying to find the best path to reach the city, they were confronted by the Mexican troops at the Battle of Padierna. The Mexicans occupied the high ground, and they saw initial success, but they could not finish off the Americans due to the lack of reinforcements. After being surprised by the Mexicans at night, the vanguard retreated but, with a coordinated assault in the morning of August 20th, managed to drive the Mexican forces away. The Americans then pushed farther northwest, encountering another fortified Mexican position at Churubusco, which they managed to take thanks to their artillery. With the victories at Padierna and Churubusco, it was apparent that Scott had the edge. They had established their position south of the city and planned to advance on it next. Santa Anna started preparing for one final stand.[124]

To the southwest of Mexico City was Chapultepec, an old castle that also doubled as a military school, which was situated on a hill. Chapultepec was a very difficult but valuable location to take. Actually, seizing the castle on top of the hill would require a lot of effort, in turn providing vast control over the area near Mexico City. Despite the fact that it was not directly in the way to taking Mexico City, Scott knew that Santa Anna had a part of his force ready to defend it. If the Americans chose to ignore it, then their flank would have been open during the main siege of the city.

---

[124] Heidler (2006), pp. 127-130.

That is why on September 8ᵗʰ, Scott's forces started attacking the Mexican troops that were defending the road to Chapultepec. This proved to be a costly action for Scott since the Mexican artillery, which had largely been ineffective in the past, was firing freely on the Americans from above. In the skirmish, the Americans managed to break the Mexicans who defended the road to Chapultepec but suffered heavy casualties. Five days later, after regrouping and carefully assessing the situation, Scott's main army, now that they had gained access, assembled at the castle and started heavily bombarding it. Not a lot of Mexicans were actually defending the castle, and they were overwhelmed by the determined American forces.[125] When storming the castle, Scott's men completely wiped out the Mexicans. Among the fallen were the famous six cadets of the military academy— mere teenagers whose deaths became "a symbol and image of this unrighteous war."[126] With Chapultepec, Scott had clear access to the capital.

The main American offensive on Mexico City came onto the gates of Belén and San Cosmé. Scott's division had a relatively easy time entering the city. The defenders at the Belén gate had retreated without putting up a fight due to a lack of ammunition. While the San Cosmé gate was better defended, it was quickly taken by the Americans with their artillery and help from the division that had taken the Belén gate. Scott, however, halted his advance for a bit, hoping to receive some kind of peace offer; he also knew that the fighting inside the city would be costly.

However, for Santa Anna, the situation was doomed. That night, he made the decision to flee the city with the generals loyal to him and some nine thousand soldiers. The final trick up the abandoning *caudillo*'s sleeve was opening up the prison cells and releasing thousands of prisoners onto the streets of Mexico City to make it as difficult for Scott to subdue the situation as possible. Despite all this,

---

[125] Heidler (2006), pp. 130-133.

[126] Heidler (2006), p. 33.

Scott officially claimed Mexico City for the United States on September 14th. After a campaign that had lasted for about eight months, Scott had finally taken the Mexican capital, putting an end to major fighting between the two nations. Peace, however, was yet to be secured.

A lithograph of the US occupation of Mexico City by Adolphe Jean-Baptiste Bayot (Source: Wikimedia Commons)

The All Mexico Movement and the Treaty of Guadalupe Hidalgo

When Scott occupied the capital, the United States' victory became clearer than ever to the Mexican doubters who still had some hope of turning things around in the war. The American campaign was an obvious success. Polk had managed to overcome any challenge Mexico threw at him on three different occasions. First, he managed to defeat them near the disputed Rio Grande border. Then, although in a bit more disoriented way, the US took control over Santa Fe and California. And, finally, due to the brilliance of General Scott and the determination of his army, as well as the inability of Santa Anna to put up a proper defense, the US forces infiltrated the heart of Mexico and got hold of its capital—a feat that had not been achieved since the Spanish under Hernán Cortés. All of this was a thorn in the side of an already struggling Mexico.

Despite occupying Mexico City in September of 1847, the two sides did not officially sign a peace treaty until much later. The reason behind this was that after Santa Anna abandoned the city, nobody was left who wished to be identified with the defeat.[127] Yes, he had technically left the former foreign affairs minister Manuel de la Peña y Peña as the interim president, but, as one would expect, he did not have popular support. For months, Scott and Trist, who still had the responsibility of negotiating a peace deal, struggled to meet with an official government that would, at least somewhat accurately, represent the country.

One interesting factor that also played a big role in Polk's decision to choose the peace terms was the so-called All Mexico Movement. Back in the US, now that it was apparent that the territorial gains were far beyond what Polk had vouched for at the beginning of the war, many supported the idea of conquering all of Mexico. They knew that the Mexicans did not possess the power to oppose the US. The All Mexico Movement was supported mostly by those slave-owning Democrats who had always been fierce advocates of expansion; they saw the conquered lands as a way of enriching their slave numbers. The Wilmot Proviso—a proposal in Congress in 1846 to ban slavery in all lands acquired from the Mexican-American War—was unsuccessful, giving even more power to the All Mexico Movement. The phenomenon was one of the most extreme manifestations of Manifest Destiny, calling to forcefully incorporate millions of people and the lands where they dwelled into the United States.[128]

---

[127] Suchlicki (1996), p. 77.

[128] Heidler (2006), p. 136.

The All Mexico Movement was also met with strong opposition. Among the people who spoke up against the idea of conquering all of Mexico was, of course, John Quincy Adams, a veteran in opposing any decisions that would allow slave-owners to expand their power. Adams believed that if the United States claimed all of the Mexican territories, the slave states would become more powerful, thus shifting the balance in their favor. Many northeastern abolitionists sided with Adams. John C. Calhoun was another prominent figure who opposed the All Mexico Movement. However, unlike Adams, Calhoun was a slave-owning Whig who preferred subtle expansion and thought that acquiring all of the Mexican territories would incorporate many racially inferior people into the United States. Furthermore, those who, in general, did not support the war since the beginning saw the All Mexico Movement as deeply immoral. After all, the United States should have been the spreader of peace (something that, in their eyes, was already violated with the war), and annexing a whole independent country would not be appropriate.

All in all, it was clear for Polk that he needed to come up with a peace treaty that would at least try to please the majority. The war was won, but just how much territory would the United States acquire from it? Polk's initial intentions were to just secure Texas and California, something that his armies had already accomplished. Scott's campaign to Mexico City was, in fact, mostly caused due to the Mexicans' reluctance to negotiate for peace after losing those territories. Who knows; perhaps if they had negotiated before General Scott started his long march from Veracruz to Mexico City, many hardships may have been avoided. As it stood, however, Polk could not just annex all of Mexico and hope for the best. The sociopolitical issues that would arise all throughout the country would cause many problems. He also could not just take his original goals of Texas and California, as that would leave the New Mexico region awkwardly stuck between the American territories. Thus, Polk came up with the following.

When Nicholas Trist finally met with Mexican officials Luis G. Cuevas, Bernardo Couto, and Miguel Atristain on February 2nd, 1848, in the small village of Guadalupe Hidalgo to negotiate peace, the two sides signed a treaty that would be ratified on May 30th. According to the treaty, Mexico agreed to recognize Texas as a lawful part of the United States, giving up all its claims. In addition, the new border was officially established from the mouth of the Rio Grande all the way to New Mexico and then westward to California, just south of San Diego. Mexico lost one-third of all its territory. The United States, in turn, gained a huge chunk of land of about 520,000 miles—an area larger than Spain, France, and Italy combined. All the citizens who lived in the acquired territories were given the right to choose their citizenship. Last but not least, the United States paid an amount of $15 million for these territories, as well as for all the damages that it may have caused during the war.[129]

The Treaty of Guadalupe Hidalgo was a historic decision. It marked the official end of the Mexican-American War, a conflict that cost the lives of more than thirteen thousand people. It also marked the end of a difficult chapter for both countries. The next chapter for the United States and Mexico would prove to be just as tumultuous as the one before it, filled with instability, internal bickering, and the lust for power.

---

[129] Miller (1996), p. 229.

Chapter 7 – Postwar US and Mexico

The Effects of the War on Mexico

The war had a devastating effect on Mexico, which had already been in a difficult state since independence. The Mexican Army, despite it being more sizable than that of the United States, just could not match the opposition. It mostly consisted of poorly trained and demoralized conscripts, most of whom were of Native American descent. They had worse guns and equipment, which were outdated by the time the fighting between the two nations broke out.[130] Due to this, it comes as no surprise that Mexico did not really achieve any substantial victories throughout the course of the war. It was an almost impossible task to make millions of men, who were already troubled with various problems of their own in the country, fight against the professionally trained, well-armed soldiers of the ambitious United States, which arguably had the most advanced military at the time. Desertion became a prominent problem in the ranks of the Mexicans; the soldiers knew that they were marching to their deaths, so they chose to flee instead of facing it headfirst.

---

[130] Suchlicki (1996), p. 77.

Thus, the defeat was a logical result. Santa Anna retired and went into exile once again. As for the nation, the loss of so many lives and such a sizable portion of their territory was a psychological blow, which would exist for many years. The United States had humiliated Mexico about ten years after Texas had managed to do so. Due to this, a deep feeling of "Yankeephobia," a manifestation of hatred and fear toward the American people, was rooted deep into the minds of the Mexican people.[131] In Mexico, the war is known as the "War of North American Invasion" rather than the Mexican-American War.[132]

Plus, ultimately, such devastation could have been theoretically avoided, or the issue could have been handled in a better way. This is not to say that Mexico ever had a realistic chance of decisively defeating the US. Instead, they could have chosen to avoid the imminent war by giving up their claims over the Rio Grande border, which was the issue that initially started the conflict. However, the sense of pride that Mexico embraced so much, as well as the inability to competently act in times of danger, resulted in the Mexican people trusting an old, cunning leader who, instead of leading them to victory, led them to their tragic demise. A part of the country did blame the loss of the war entirely on Santa Anna, and rightfully so, but when chaos ensued in the immediate years following the war, they still could not resist one final return of the *caudillo*.

After the war, both liberals and conservatives blamed each other for the defeat. The conservatives believed that the country's right path lay in the reinstitution of the monarchy, possibly with a competent European ruler who would be able to use their influence and experience to bring about the period of peace that the people of Mexico dreamed of. They also advocated for restoring the powers to the Catholic Church, another institution they hoped could unite the people. The liberals, on the other hand, strongly opposed any of those proposals. They argued that it was the church and the legally

---

[131] Miller (1996), p. 229.

[132] Suchlicki (1996), p. 78.

obscure administrative units of Mexico that caused the army's incompetence and their failure in the war. The liberals believed that they should be heavily reformed to ensure the country's future safety.

In the wake of all this chaos, Santa Anna made his final return in 1853, when he was made perpetual dictator of Mexico. Together with the head of his cabinet, the conservative leader Lucas Alamán, Santa Anna wished for the economic revival of the country. The first reforms of the duo included the development of the country's outdated infrastructure and telegraph lines to better connect the people of Mexico. This caused more and more people to start living in previously unoccupied lands. Although Santa Anna had initial success, with the sudden death of Lucas Alamán, he had no one to restrain him. Thus, instead of focusing on civic projects and the further improvement of his people's quality of life, he increased the size of the army, paying a fortune to bring commanders from Europe to train his men. He began spending the federal reserves and took excessive loans to finance his projects. Ironically, this resulted in him selling the Mesilla Valley territory—a portion of land in modern-day New Mexico—to the United States. He sold the territory for about $10 million, but he did not use the money to repay his loans. He continued to spend lavishly, upsetting his people even more.[133]

This period of turmoil would continue in the country until 1855, when Santa Anna was deposed by the rebelling liberals who were fed up with the *caudillo*'s efforts to repress them. They were led by a pure-blooded Zapotec from Oaxaca called Benito Juárez. He would dominate Mexican history for the next twenty years, first by establishing a liberal government and implementing a series of reforms that helped the Mexican people, and then by leading the struggle against the brief French occupation of Mexico in the 1860s.[134] His success story, from a low-born Zapotec to a visionary that wanted the best for his country, inspired countless people to join the effort of

---

[133] Suchlicki (1996), pp. 79-80.

[134] Miller (1996), p. 231.

making Mexico a better place for everyone. It would be Juárez who would form the basis of the democratic republic that is Mexico today, reforming the country and promoting the principles of private property, as well as social and judicial equality.

These are just some of the major developments in Mexico after the war. The troubled but at the same time odd history of Mexico after the war also included a small period of time when it was controlled by the French monarch Maximilian—something that can be considered as an anomaly in the grand scheme of things. All in all, however, the defeat left the Mexicans divided, and the years that followed saw them slowly disintegrate into more and more chaos until individuals like Benito Juárez took the initiative. On the one hand, the early history of Mexico, starting from its independence up to the Mexican-American War, can be described by just one name: Santa Anna. On the other hand, the legacy that it left is regarded by the Mexicans as a tragedy where countless people lost their lives in the midst of internal fighting and instability.

The Postwar United States

The United States had managed to win the war with relative ease. To be fair, there was little doubt in the minds of proud Americans that they would ever be defeated in any type of conflict against Mexico. The main problem throughout the course of the war was whether or not it should have been fought in the first place and, after winning (because it was almost guaranteed), which territory the country should have seized, if any. President Polk's approach to the existing border disputes with Mexico was to take control over the disputed territory up to the Rio Grande, and it certainly did not include capturing the provinces of New Mexico and California through a war. Polk did plan to eventually integrate California into the US, just as he had done with Oregon, but he never wanted to go to war with Mexico over it. That is why he did not answer the calls of those who pushed for "All Mexico." In the span of his four very successful years as president, he managed to accomplish what he had asserted during his presidential campaign. He had annexed Texas and secured its border; made Oregon an official American territory, ending joint-control with the British; and seized the "promised land" of California (with the added benefit of the massive New Mexico territory). His presidency was a success, and it was the peak of Manifest Destiny.

Seeing that the war had been such a success, Polk wanted to send troops to the Mexican province of Yucatán to help them with their rebellion. Justifying his wish of interfering to Congress with the Monroe Doctrine and claiming that Yucatán could have been potentially occupied by Europeans (as Spain and Great Britain had also been approached by the Yucatán for aid), Polk proposed that the US troops in the province should dissuade the Europeans from taking any actions. This proposal was almost instantly rejected by Congress, which had grown tired of hearing about sending American soldiers to Mexico. The opposition, led by John C. Calhoun, reminded Polk that the United States had never intervened in Latin America, saying that if the newly born South American countries were willing to send forces to help Yucatán, then they would have requested the same aid for themselves.[135] Polk's final effort to expand was to acquire another valuable territory in the region—the island of Cuba, which was still under Spanish rule. It was the only major island in the Caribbean where slavery was actively practiced, with over 300,000 slaves living there at the end of the 1840s. Had it been successful, the consequences from the acquisition of Cuba might have been game-changing. It would have likely been one of the strongest additions to the slave states, shifting the balance heavily in favor of those who advocated for the practice. However, despite Polk's efforts to purchase it, Spain refused to sell.[136]

Despite this, the Americans still had their long-standing dream of stretching their glorious country from the Atlantic to the Pacific

---

[135] LaFeber (1994), pp. 121-122.

[136] LaFeber (1994), p. 123.

realized. Due to these new lands, they started migrating westward to get away from the busy cities and to own small parcels of land. There, they would fulfill the potential of the lands that the "inferior" Mexicans had failed to achieve. However, as many had predicted, they failed to realize what this sudden expansion meant for a country that was already politically torn internally. Polk acquired an enormous portion of land for the US, but it was the newly elected president, the war hero Zachary Taylor, who had to deal with the issue of how to govern them.

At that point, the issue of slavery had been haunting everyone in the country. The two sides opposed each other in everything. What made the issue even more confusing was that the slavery divide was not solely based on party preferences. Even though, generally, the Democrats were considered to be anti-slavery, there were many who were pro-slavery, and many Whigs, in return, opposed it. All of this caused further internal party divides between the factions. What was agreed between the sides was that the balance between the slave and free states should be maintained. The 1820 Missouri Compromise and any other efforts to draw hypothetical geographical lines to determine where slavery was to be legal were no longer relevant. The Wilmot Proviso had failed. What made matters even more complicated was that gold was discovered in California in 1848, causing the region to be flooded with settlers who came from all over the country and even the world. So, when California applied to join the Union in 1849, it had a large enough population to instantly apply as a state, skipping territorial status. Its inhabitants had already chosen to prohibit the practice of slavery, urging Congress to come up with a solution to deal with its integration in a way that would upset those who were pro-slavery.[137]

---

[137] Heidler (2006), p. 144.

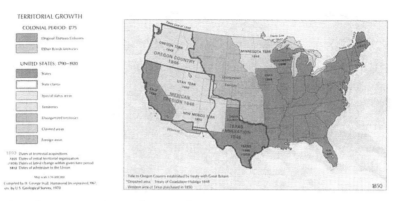

What the United States looked like by 1850. (Source: Wikimedia Commons)

Thus was born one of the greatest debates in US history, which produced the Compromise of 1850. Henry Clay would come up with a plan that would try to satisfy both sides. According to the plan, which was eventually adopted by Congress, California would enter the Union as a free state, upsetting the balance between the number of free and slave states in the country. In addition, Texas would cede a part of its territory—fixing its boundary to what it is today—which, in turn, exempted it from its debt that would amount to almost $10 million. The territories that would be ceded by Texas would be established as part of the territories of New Mexico and Utah, and they would have the option of deciding whether or not they would adopt slavery once they applied to join the Union. Furthermore, the compromise would prohibit the slave trade (not the practice of slavery itself) in the District of Columbia—an embarrassing feat that Clay believed was not fit for the capital of the country. Finally, under the proposed Fugitive Slave Act, it would be the federal government's responsibility to return all the slaves who would escape in the future to their rightful owners.[138]

[138] Urofsky, M. I. (2021, June 7). "Compromise of 1850." Encyclopedia Britannica. https://www.britannica.com/event/Compromise-of-1850.

Even though the Compromise of 1850 pacified both sides for the time being, it was not enough to ensure stability in the long term. The system that was in place was always doomed to fail. The differences between the two sides could not have coexisted in a healthy environment, and everything, including foreign policy, had an impact. Ultimately, this was something that many people, including President Polk, failed to realize. He always focused on his "mission" to expand the boundaries of his country and fulfill the destiny of the American people that was ordained to them by the heavens. Ignoring the slavery issue for years caused it to slowly grow and fester behind the scenes. Eventually, it would become something that would tear the country apart with the Civil War and cost the lives of hundreds of thousands of Americans in the process.

These were the effects of the Mexican-American War. Polk's inability to acknowledge the fact that foreign and internal affairs were intertwined caused perhaps the most tragic war in the history of the United States. The US stood victorious from its first major offensive war, despite it being masked as a defensive one in the beginning. However, what would follow would be a society divided more than ever on a matter that still remains a sensitive issue today. The age of avoiding the slave question was over with the end of the Mexican-American War. The results of the Mexican-American War would help light the spark that would cause the country to descend into the Civil War.

Conclusion

The Mexican-American War remains one of the most influential, albeit less known, wars in North American history. It affected the lives of the millions of people who lived in both countries. More than anything, it had a massive cultural impact that is still seen today. For instance, modern-day US states that border Mexico are still largely inhabited by a Spanish-speaking Latino population.

Ultimately, the war had dire consequences, causing further instability in both Mexico and the US. Many actors of the Civil War—the conflict that would eventually overshadow the Mexican-American War because of its historical significance—also participated in the events mentioned above.

All in all, while the Mexicans considered themselves as tragic victims of US aggression, the people in the United States believed that they had finally achieved the dream of stretching their country to its rightful borders. The Mexican-American War shaped the political geography of the continent and laid foundations for the paths the two countries would take in the future.

Here's another book by Captivating History that you might like

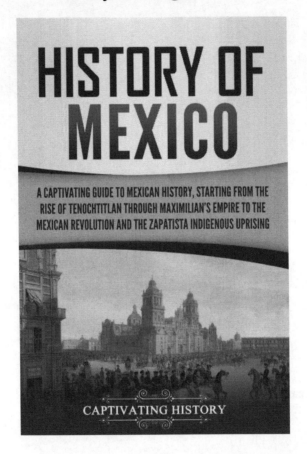

Free Bonus from Captivating History (Available for a Limited time)

Hi History Lovers!

Now you have a chance to join our exclusive history list so you can get your first history ebook for free as well as discounts and a potential to get more history books for free! Simply visit the link below to join.

Captivatinghistory.com/ebook

Also, make sure to follow us on Facebook, Twitter and Youtube by searching for Captivating History.

References

Delay, Brian. (2007). "Independent Indians and the U.S.-Mexican War." The American Historical Review, 112(1), 35–68. http://www.jstor.org/stable/4136006.

"Viceroyalty of New Spain (historical territory, Mexico)." Encyclopedia Britannica. Retrieved 14 October, 2021.

Parry, J. H. (1940). "The Audiencia of New Galicia in the Sixteenth Century." Cambridge Historical Journal, 6(3), 263–282. http://www.jstor.org/stable/3020752.

L. N. Mcalister. "Social Structure and Social Change in New Spain." Hispanic American Historical Review 1 August 1963; 43 (3): 349–370. doi: https://doi.org/10.1215/00182168-43.3.349

[Anon.] (2001). "Sociolinguistic stratification in New Spain." 2001 (149), 55-78. https://doi.org/10.1515/ijsl.2001.023

Palfrey, Dale Hoyt. (1998). "Religion and society in New Spain: Mexico's Colonial era." Retrieved from https://www.mexconnect.com/articles/1562-religion-and-society-in-new-spain-mexico-s-colonial-era/.

Cañeque, Alejandro. *The King's Living Image: The Culture and Politics of Viceregal Power in Colonial Mexico.* New York: Routledge, 2004.

Von Wobeser, Gisela. "La consolidación de vales reales como factor determinante de la lucha de independencia en México, 1804-1808." Historia mexicana (2006).

David E. Narrett. (2012). "Geopolitics and Intrigue: James Wilkinson, the Spanish Borderlands, and Mexican Independence." The William and Mary Quarterly, 69(1), 101-146. https://doi.org/10.5309/willmaryquar.69.1.0101.

Guedea, Virginia. "The First Popular Elections in Mexico City, 1812-1813" in the Evolution of the Mexican Political System. Jaime E. Rodríguez O., ed. Wilmington: Scholarly Resources 1993.

Russell, P. (2011). *The History of Mexico: From Pre-conquest to Present.* Routledge.

Wolf, E. R. (1958). "The Virgin of Guadalupe: A Mexican National Symbol." The Journal of American Folklore, 71(279), 34-39. https://doi.org/10.2307/537957

Anna, T. E. (1996). "Inventing Mexico: Provincehood and Nationhood after Independence." Bulletin of Latin American Research, 15(1), 7-17. http://www.jstor.org/stable/3339401.

Wolf, E. R., & Hansen, E. C. (1967). "Caudillo Politics: A Structural Analysis." Comparative Studies in Society and History, 9(2), 168-179. http://www.jstor.org/stable/177739.

Krauze, E. (1997). *Mexico: Biography of Power.* New York: HarperCollins.

Fowler, W. (2007). *Santa Anna of Mexico.* University of Nebraska Press.

Oxford English Dictionary. "Filibuster." Retrieved October 14, 2021.

Rodriguez, S. K. M. (2017). "'The Greatest Nation on Earth': The Politics and Patriotism of the First Anglo American Immigrants to Mexican Texas, 1820-1824." Pacific Historical Review, 86(1), 50-83. https://www.jstor.org/stable/26419727.

Shadle, Stan. "Review of The First Century of Mexican Independence, by Ward S. Albro, Leslie Bethell, Helen Delpar, Michael C. Meyer, William L. Sherman, Allen Peskin, Jasper Ridley, et al." Latin American Research Review 31, no. 1 (1996): 244-58. http://www.jstor.org/stable/2503860.

Bennet, M. S. (1899). "The Battle of Gonzales, the 'Lexington' of the Texas Revolution." The Quarterly of the Texas State Historical Association, 2(4), 313-316. http://www.jstor.org/stable/30242776.

Davis, W. C. (2017). *Lone Star Rising*. Simon and Schuster.

Haynes, S.W., Saxon, G.D., Cantrell, G., Schlereth, E., Haynes, S.W., & Soto, M. (2015). *Contested Empire: Rethinking the Texas Revolution*. College Station: Texas A&M University Press.

Jeffries, C. (1942). "The Lights of the Alamo." The Southwestern Historical Quarterly, 46(1), 1-8. http://www.jstor.org/stable/30240588.

Winters, J. W. (1902). "An Account of the Battle of San Jacinto." The Quarterly of the Texas State Historical Association, 6(2), 139-144. http://www.jstor.org/stable/27784928.

Diaz, M. A. (2016). "To Conquer the Coast: Pensacola, the Gulf of Mexico, and the Construction of American Imperialism, 1820-1848." The Florida Historical Quarterly, 95(1), 1-25. http://www.jstor.org/stable/24769295.

LaFeber, W. (1994). *The American Age: United States Foreign Policy at Home and Abroad since 1750* (2nd ed.). Norton.

Britannica, T. Editors of Encyclopedia (2019, October 21). "Transcontinental Treaty." Encyclopedia Britannica. https://www.britannica.com/event/Transcontinental-Treaty

Paterson, T. G. (2005). Major Problems in American Foreign Relations: Documents and Essays. (D. Merrill, Ed.) (Sixth, Ser. Major problems in American history series). Houghton Mifflin.

Britannica, T. Editors of Encyclopedia (2021, August 18). "Monroe Doctrine." Encyclopedia Britannica. https://www.britannica.com/event/Monroe-Doctrine

Merk, F., & Merk, L. B. (1995). *Manifest Destiny and Mission in American History: A Reinterpretation* (1st Harvard University Press paperback). Harvard University Press.

Baigell, M. (1990). "Territory, Race, Religion: Images of Manifest Destiny." Smithsonian Studies in American Art, 4(3/4), 3-21. http://www.jstor.org/stable/3109013.

Miller, R. R. (1996). *Mexico: A History.* University of Oklahoma Press.

Suchlicki, J. (1996). *Mexico: From Montezuma to NAFTA, Chiapas, and Beyond.* Brassey's.

"Cuartelazo." Encyclopedia of Latin American History and Culture. Retrieved October 27, 2021 from Encyclopedia.com: https://www.encyclopedia.com/humanities/encyclopedias-almanacs-transcripts-and-maps/cuartelazo

Bethell, L. (1991). *Mexico since Independence (The Cambridge History of Latin America).* Cambridge University Press.

Fulmore, Z. T. (1901). "The Annexation of Texas and the Mexican War." The Quarterly of the Texas State Historical Association, 5(1), 28-48. http://www.jstor.org/stable/27784897.

Smith, J. H. (1910). "The Mexican Recognition of Texas." The American Historical Review, 16(1), 36-55. https://doi.org/10.2307/1834307

Barker, E. C. (1946). "The Annexation of Texas." The Southwestern Historical Quarterly, 50(1), 49-74. http://www.jstor.org/stable/30237259.

Osborn, C. (2015). "The Changing Mexico-US Border." The Library of Congress. https://blogs.loc.gov/maps/2015/12/the-changing-mexico-u-s-border/.

Heidler, D. S., Heidler, J. T., & Greenwood Press. (2006). *The Mexican War* (Ser. Greenwood Guides to Historic Events, 1500-1900). Greenwood Press.

Lawrence, N. (2013). "'This boa-constrictor appetite of swallowing states and provinces': Anti-Imperialist Opposition to the U.S./Mexican War." South Central Review, 30(1), 55–82. http://www.jstor.org/stable/44016818.

Widger, D. (2018). "Memoirs of General U. S. Grant." https://www.gutenberg.org/files/4367/4367-h/4367-h.htm

Walker, D. L. (1999). *Bear Flag Rising: The Conquest of California, 1846.* New York: Forge.

Urofsky, M. I. (2021, June 7). "Compromise of 1850." Encyclopedia Britannica. https://www.britannica.com/event/Compromise-of-1850.

Printed in Great Britain
by Amazon